C000099013

THE CONFUCIAN WORLD OBSERVED

THE CONFUCIAN WORLD OBSERVED

A Contemporary Discussion of Confucian Humanism in East Asia

Edited by

Tu Weiming
Milan Hejtmanek
Alan Wachman

Program for Cultural Studies
The East-West Center • Honolulu, Hawaii

Copyright © 1992 The East-West Center
All rights reserved
Manufactured in the United States of America

Third Printing, 1994

ISBN 0-8248-1451-7

*The paper used in this publication meets the
minimum requirements of American National
Standard for Information Sciences—Permanence
of Paper for Printed Library Materials*

Camera-ready copy for this book was prepared
by the Program for Cultural Studies,
East-West Center

Distributed by
University of Hawaii Press
Order Department
2840 Kolowalu Street
Honolulu, Hawaii 96822

Contents

Preface

THE PURPOSE of the workshop on Confucian humanism was to explore Confucian ethics as a common intellectual discourse in East Asia from a multidisciplinary and cross-cultural perspective. Scholars in the humanities and social sciences who specialize in the region (mainland China, Japan, South Korea, Taiwan, Hong Kong, and Singapore), as well as scholars in comparative civilizational studies, participated in nine intensive sessions. Discussion focused on how the Confucian ethic has worked in shaping perceptions of selfhood, dynamics of familial relations, gender construction, social organization, political authority, popular beliefs, and economic culture in East Asia.

As an integral part of the American Academy of Arts and Sciences project to understand "The Rise of East Asia," the workshop examined the assumption that Confucian humanism is a shared value system—an underlying grammar of action and a common language of "communicative rationality"—in Japan and the Four Mini-Dragons. Instead of confirming or rejecting the assumption, the participants debated the claim that Confucian ethics, as reflected in government leadership, competitive education, meritocratic elitism, social interaction, a disciplined work force, principles of equality and self-reliance, and self-cultivation, provides a necessary background and a powerful motivating force for the rise of industrial East Asia—the most dynamic region of sustained economic growth and political development since the Second World War.

While the so-called post-Confucian hypothesis loomed large in the minds of the participants, the workshop did not directly address the issue (as framed by Peter Berger in *In Search of an East Asian Development Model*) of whether "a key variable in explaining the economic performance of these countries is Confucian ethics." Rather, by focusing on the Confucian values and their institutional embodiments, the workshop offered thought-provoking interpretations of the life-orientations of the cultural elite and the general populace in Japan and the Four Mini-Dragons.

A subsequent phase of the Academy Project, directed by Ezra Vogel of Harvard University, will focus on Japan's global impact in economic, scientific, political, military, and cultural terms. Because of its economic dynamism, Japan merits special attention. The intriguing phenomenon of the rise of industrial East Asia has been variously labeled "The Sinic World in Perspective" (Edwin Reischauer, 1974), "Japan as Number One" (Ezra Vogel, 1979), "The Emerging Japanese Superstate" (Herman Kahn, 1979), "The Post-Confucian Challenge" (Roderick MacFarquhar, 1980), "The Japanese Miracle" (Chalmers Johnson, 1982), "The Eastasia Edge" (Hofheinz and Calder, 1982), and "An East Asian Development Model" (Peter Berger, 1988). How to locate Japan culturally remains a fascinating issue. "Japanese exceptionalism" serves as a constant warning to avoid facile generalizations about the Sinic world or the Confucian universe. Our study will examine the rise of East Asia as a complex whole, in terms of both its traditional roots and their modern transformations throughout the region.

The events of the student demonstration at Tiananmen Square were folding during the workshop and lent significance to a key question: To what extent can Confucian humanism creatively transform itself into a communal critical self-awareness of the Chinese intelligentsia without losing sight of its moral demands for public service and political participation? Indeed, the far-reaching implications of the role and function of Confucian institutions in industrial East Asia for mainland China and the modern West will be studied in the future as integral parts of this Academy project.

Acknowledgments

THE RAPPORTEUR of the Workshop on Confucian Humanism, Alan Wachman, wrote a summary of the workshop discussions for the *Bulletin of the American Academy of Arts and Sciences* (March 1990). Subsequently, Milan Hejtmanek, another rapporteur, went through the recorded material and produced a narrative of the conversation, capturing in some detail the flow of the three-day discussion. The editors then met regularly for several months to reflect upon the manuscript section by section. In the summer of 1990, Mr. Hejtmanek spent two weeks at the East-West Center to complete the draft for publication.

Tu Weiming's introductory note to the aforementioned Academy report is presented here as the preface to this volume, and Wachman's summary, titled "The Confucian Problematique: An Overview," follows as chapter 1. The titles of the other chapters were topics originally assigned to and arranged for the workshop. With the exception of Professor Peter Bol's intervention on pages 18–20, which is excerpted from a written communication he later sent us, the digested conversation is based solely on the presumed "faithful interpretation" of the editors. We are, therefore, responsible for any mistaken or misleading synopses of the participants' points of view.

We are grateful to Mr. David Chu (Zhu Xiaokang) for his proofreading, to Professor Fran Conroy for his work on the index, and to Ms. Chen Xia and Mr. Yang Tsung Rong for their help in preparing the glossary. This publication, supported by the project on the cultural dimension of Asian development under the directorship of Professor Robert Dernberger of the University of Michigan at Ann Arbor, is financed by a generous grant from Laurance and Mary Rockefeller to enable the East-West Center to take new initiatives in cultural studies. We thank Dr. Charles Morrison, coordinator of the Center's International Relations Program, for making these funds available to us.

The observers of the workshop, notably Eske Møllgaard, Sara Queen, and Cathy Wang, all Ph.D. candidates in East Asian studies at Harvard, have engaged us in a continuous conversation on Confucian humanism. As questions of democracy, civil society, human rights, and due process of law loom large in the minds of the Chinese intellectuals in the post-Tiananmen era, the need to extend the scope of the Confucian discourse beyond the confines of the scholarly community becomes obvious. We are indebted to Mrs. Corinne Schelling of the Academy and Dr. Terry Lautz of the Luce Foundation for making the workshop possible in the first place and to colleagues at the East-West Center for allowing the conversation to assume a more tangible form.

Participants in the
Workshop on Confucian Humanism

PETER L. BERGER is director of the Institute for the Study of Economic Culture and professor for the University Professors Program at Boston University, Boston, Massachusetts.

JOHN BERTHRONG is associate dean of the School of Theology at Boston University, Boston, Massachusetts.

PETER K. BOL is professor of Chinese history at Harvard University, Cambridge, Massachusetts.

CHANG HAO is professor of history at The Ohio State University, Columbus, Ohio.

GEORGE DE VOS is professor emeritus in the Department of Anthropology, University of California, Berkeley.

RONALD DORE is visiting professor in the Department of Political Science, Massachusetts Institute of Technology, Cambridge, Massachusetts.

CARTER J. ECKERT is associate professor of Korean history at Harvard University, Cambridge, Massachusetts.

THOMAS GOLD is associate professor of sociology and chairman of the Center for Chinese Studies, University of California, Berkeley.

STEPHEN GRAUBARD is editor of *Daedalus,* American Academy of Arts and Sciences, Cambridge, Massachusetts.

MILAN HEJTMANEK is a Ph.D. candidate in the Committee on History and East Asian Languages, Harvard University, Cambridge, Massachusetts.

MICHAEL KALTON is professor of religion at Wichita State University, Wichita, Kansas.

KIM HYUNG-GYUN is a Ph.D. candidate in the School of Theology at Boston University, Boston, Massachusetts.

KIM KWANG-OK is professor of anthropology at Seoul National University, Seoul, Korea.

TERRILL LAUTZ is with the Henry Luce Foundation.

LIN TONGQI is associate professor of English at Beijing University of Foreign Studies, Beijing, China, and an associate of the Department of East Asian Languages and Civilizations at Harvard University, Cambridge, Massachusetts.

RODERICK MACFARQUHAR is Leroy B. Williams Professor of History and Political Science and director of the John King Fairbank Center for East Asian Research at Harvard University, Cambridge, Massachusetts.

RICHARD MADSEN is professor of sociology at the University of California, San Diego.

HENRY ROSOVSKY is Lewis P. and Linda L. Geyser University Professor and acting dean of the Faculty of Arts and Sciences, Harvard University, Cambridge, Massachusetts.

GILBERT ROZMAN is professor of sociology at Princeton University, Princeton, New Jersey.

BENJAMIN I. SCHWARTZ is Leroy B. Williams Professor of History and Political Science (Emeritus), John King Fairbank Center for East Asian Research, Harvard University, Cambridge, Massachusetts.

JOANNA F. HANDLIN SMITH is associate editor of the *Harvard Journal of Asiatic Studies* and an associate in research at the John King Fairbank Center for East Asian Research, Harvard University, Cambridge, Massachusetts.

TU WEIMING is director of the Institute of Culture and Communication, East-West Center, Honolulu, Hawaii, and professor of Chinese history and philosophy at Harvard University, Cambridge, Massachusetts.

EZRA VOGEL is Henry Ford II Professor of Social Sciences in the Department of Sociology at Harvard University, Cambridge, Massachusetts.

ALAN WACHMAN is a Ph.D. candidate in the Department of Government, Harvard University, Cambridge, Massachusetts.

WANG GUNGWU is vice chancellor of Hong Kong University.

JAMES WATSON is John King and Wilma Cannon Fairbank Professor of Chinese Society at Harvard University in Cambridge, Massachusetts.

SAMUEL YAMASHITA is associate professor of history at Pomona College in Claremont, California.

The Confucian Problematique: An Overview

IN EACH SESSION of the workshop on Confucian humanism, the participants considered the role of Confucian institutions in contemporary East Asia by addressing an ostensibly distinct realm of social interaction. Despite their efforts to identify and articulate the influence of Confucian values on the structure and operation of specific social, political, spiritual, or economic institutions, certain underlying concerns surfaced repeatedly and linked the discussions in each session to common refrains throughout the conference.

The primary concern was whether there is justification in characterizing contemporary East Asia as Confucian. Each participant attempted to assert an acceptable definition of what is Confucian from the perspective of the culture he knows best and the discipline in which he studies. Not only was consensus elusive, but at times the debate turned on the term *Confucian* itself and whether it describes anything other than the texts written by Confucius and his disciples. Some even raised the challenging question of whether Confucianism—a system of ideas founded on Confucian values—is real or merely imagined by scholars to enable them to speak with each other about their perceptions.

The second set of concerns pertained to the role Confucian institutions play in contemporary East Asia—an inquiry predicated on the assertion that such institutions exist. Participants who accepted the validity of Confucianism as a social force were urged to describe its influence and to differentiate Confucian values from others that affect East Asian social institutions. Ultimately, the failure to identify explicitly the specific Confucian contributions reflected competing notions about the nature of the conceptual beast under consideration.

A third theme, subordinate to the first two, flowed from Max Weber's observations about the deleterious effects of Confucian values on China's economic development as compared with the effects of the Protestant work ethic on the West. The conferees debated whether Confucian values have impeded or accelerated the processes of modernization and development and discussed the potential benefits and hazards of those values to further growth.

The discussants decided against trying to isolate a single Confucian problematique. Some sought to differentiate between that which is Chinese and that which is Confucian and objected that the tendency to view the two as synonymous. Benjamin Schwartz commented that although Confucius wrote in the *Analects* that he was merely a transmitter of knowledge, the view Confucius provided was shaped by his emphasis on certain values selected from a wider corpus. He promoted a specific vision of society by associating certain practices as coherent and ignoring other practices with which they coexisted.

The tradition that grew from the writings of Confucius is directed both toward the behavior and attitudes of humanity in the interactions of daily life and towards the relationship of the human world and the cosmos. It is a sacred code of social behavior with spiritual and political content. It has been shaped and transmitted by the cultural elite and portrayed as a unifying system of values that both reflects their worldview and enables them to maintain their status as the arbiters of propriety.

In an effort to specify the common values that some view as Confucian, several conferees pointed to the economic successes of the Four Mini-Dragons (Hong Kong, Singapore, South Korea, and Taiwan) and questioned whether wealth and power were emphasized by the tradition out of which those states emerged. There was some agreement that the Confucian tradition itself was not primarily oriented toward the development of wealth and power but may have offered a setting conducive to the nurturing of such ambitions. For example, Confucian institutions appear to have fostered social and political attitudes that encouraged rapid economic development once the seeds of free enterprise were planted by some other means. From this perspective, Weber's sense that Confucianism did not serve as a functional equivalent of the Protestant work ethic is superficially correct. However, Weber apparently overlooked the role played by Confucian values in promoting patterns of familial and social organization that sustain and intensify the influence of capitalism.

CONFUCIAN ETHICS AS A COMMON DISCOURSE

The participants attempted to characterize the fundamental concepts arising out of a Confucian value system in each of several civilizations in order to identify unifying themes in Confucian ethical thought. The aim was not to rehearse the central ethical tenets of Confucian thought per se but to comment on the role and significance of Confucian ethics in the societies under discussion.

Michael Kalton suggested that in Korea Confucian ethics are expressed as a concern about social interaction in the human realm based on a view that a common rationality governs heaven and earth. Western rationality implies the ability to think in a linear fashion and act on those thoughts. Nature is seen as a vast mechanism that operates according to a pattern of interlocking truths that may be revealed by mathematical and scientific analysis. There is a belief that by identifying such truths, humanity may control nature and provide for itself "the good life" on earth.

By contrast, in the Korean Confucian system, nature—defined as heaven— is the manifestation of morality. The human and natural realms are linked by a moral order and one may ascertain the divine in nature through self-cultivation. This transformative process is an ongoing, lifelong endeavor that aims to heighten one's perception of the moral order and to embody it in one's actions. It is not a goal-oriented effort to know things about the natural realm as in the Western context, but a never-ending quest to be something more than what one has already become. By behaving in a manner increasingly reflective of the cosmic moral order, an individual helps to reproduce on earth the morality of heaven. Kalton observed that the Western and Korean Confucian attitudes toward nature give rise to different motives for human action.

In Japan, Confucian ethical discourse is characterized by a historical consciousness in which the past is valorized with constant reference to the future. According to Samuel Yamashita, one result is that history and the past are infused with powerful moral and political import, which are often used as a source of legitimacy by the ruling elite. Confucian thought also portrays social hierarchy as being reflective of the cosmic hierarchy. There is a distinct sense of a center or origin of legitimacy; consequently, space and geography are invested with moral and political value.

The Japanese had long viewed themselves, albeit with some discomfort, as being on the periphery of the Confucian system that had its center in China. During the Qing dynasty (1644–1911), while China was ruled by the Manchus, the Japanese usurped the role of center in their own vision of the Confucian cosmic structure and convinced themselves that they were somehow closer to the Chinese tradition than those who ruled China. Scholars gradually substituted references to Japan's past for those to China's in order to substantiate their growing sense of self-importance.

In the modern era, there has been an increasing appropriation of Confucian ethical discourse for non-Confucian issues. The family has been revived as an important model for social organization, which it was in the past; this affects both the political and commercial worlds. Political and ethical education is phrased in Confucian terms, so that most literate Japanese have some familiarity with the terms of Confucian ethics used to guide, educate, and control the population.

Richard Madsen remarked that in China, the unsettled attitude toward Confucian ethics reflects a profound sense of anguish about the past. Madsen views the central dilemma of intellectuals concerned with such issues as the conflict between Confucian ethics on one hand and the discourse about wealth and power on the other. Many worry that the dynamics of a system that promotes wealth through modern rationality will pervert and then destroy a social order long based on familial hierarchy and corporatism. This conflict is intensified by the ambiguity many Chinese intellectuals feel about the value of their own culture, which was once grand but, by comparison to the West, has apparently caused social repression and economic stagnation.

In 1988 a television series that was broadcast in China stirred up considerable intellectual, popular, and political debate. The theme of the six-part series *He shang (River elegy)* was that China's civilization (symbolized by the Yellow River) had declined. It advocated that China cast off the burden of its tradition, including the Confucian mentality, and open itself to the West (symbolized by the blue sea beyond).

This self-critical tendency of the Chinese intelligentsia emerged first during the May Fourth Movement in the second decade of this century, when the intelligentsia began to explore foreign ideas and to question the relationship between Chinese culture and China's regrettable fate. Since then, debates about the proper course for China have vacillated between extremes set by those who would renounce tradition in favor of modernity and development and those who would preserve but reform China's tradition to promote social and economic welfare.

Madsen noted that all cultures face similar threats to the family and social order, but it is not easy to speak of such issues in a cross-cultural context. The analysis of ethical issues involves a holistic way of thinking and requires extensive humanistic education, which no longer seems to be valued by most societies. Economic concerns are more easily understood because the language of economics has become an international one that is easily learned.

CULTURAL IDENTITY

Considering that there was fruitful ambiguity about what Confucian means, it was not surprising that one of the most fascinating issues discussed at the conference was what it means to be Confucian. It is difficult to know how to measure cultural identity or whether there is a threshold at which one must stop to still be identified as Confucian. Thomas Gold suggested that there is no specific set of attributes one must manifest in order to be considered Confucian, nor is being Confucian limited to a particular region, group, or political or social organization. Indeed, different aspects of the tradition are manifested to different degrees in different places. In Korea, Taiwan, and Hong Kong there has been a strengthening of certain aspects of the tradition that have been denigrated in mainland China itself.

Gilbert Rozman pointed out that even in China, views of Confucianism differ according to the level of society and the social class one considers. What one sees as Confucian in the imperial institution is not the same as what one sees among the merchant class, the intelligentsia, or the masses. Yet all are linked by reference to a common core of values.

Chang Hao added that until the end of the last century, China had been dominated by a Confucian worldview that emphasized the unity of heaven and humanity and permeated every level of human activity. When the integrity of the Chinese state was threatened by military aggression from abroad, social decay, and the infiltration of foreign ideas, the core values of Confucian order were seriously eroded, and the resulting conceptual dislocation among the intelligentsia persists today. The iconoclastic May Fourth Movement of 1919 arose when some intellectuals began to call for the radical rejection of Chinese traditions that were seen to have facilitated China's vulnerability and comparative backwardness.

This outlook has dominated China's intellectual and political debates since then and given rise to the question of cultural identity. The vehement and persistent cultural iconoclasm seen among intellectuals in China is a unique phenomenon in a world where other communities were also forced to accommodate to the sudden and conflictual introduction of foreign ideas and the intensification of the modernization process.

Peter Bol said that there is a tendency to discuss cultural identity as a reflection of past realities and to equate all of the values associated with China's traditional social and political orders with Confucianism. Bol asserted that Confucianism is a notion created in the West to define and discuss a phenomenon that existed in the past but is not synonymous with Chinese culture. Benjamin Schwartz added that there are distinct anti-Confucian trends in Chinese thought. Confucian and Chinese are distinct categories.

EDUCATION

Ezra Vogel described the examination system for selecting officials for government service, which was based on their mastery of the Confucian canon and
their embodiment of Confucian virtue. In China, the examination system
fostered a unified national culture because all candidates for office prepared by
studying the same Confucian texts. Although the original form and function
of the examination system were abolished in China in 1905, virtually all East
Asian states now have an analogous examination system for university admission. This phenomenon, which is manifested in mainland China, Taiwan,
Hong Kong, Singapore, and Japan, may be unique to East Asia.

The Confucian educational tradition and examination system reflect a
realm characterized by the hubris of moral authority: those who succeed as part
of the system view themselves, and are viewed by others, as a meritocratic elite.
Ronald Dore said that a Confucian seeks moral satisfaction from education
because that is a fulfillment of a god-given, family-given, cosmic-given potential. The instrumental use of education for fame and profit in the pursuit of
happiness and individual satisfaction conflicts with the Confucian view of life.
This has infused education in most of East Asia with an emphasis on high
standards. In addition, unlike schools in the West, which are expected to refrain
from encroaching on the duties of the family and church, schools in East Asia
are expected to instill moral values in their students; this lends a moral
dimension to the entire educational process.

Tu Weiming said that for centuries, the educational system in East Asia has
focused on a curriculum established by the neo-Confucian scholar Zhu Xi
(1130–1200). Students began by studying *The Great Learning (Daxue)*, which
focuses on the holistic links between self, family, community, and state, the
inseparability of morality and politics, and the dichotomy of inner and outer,
as manifested in self-transformation and political leadership. Then they turned
to the *Analects*, which offer commonsense notions about how to be human.
Next, students read Mencius, whose vision of self-understanding is an apologia
for intellectuals as masters of culture, as well as the basis of moral authority in
the state. Finally, they read the *Doctrine of the Mean (Zhong yong)*, which
emphasizes inner resources for cultivation.

Tu agreed with Dore that the hubris that results from this tradition is quite
powerful. Although few have been exposed during the past seventy years to the
formal training of the Four Books, the ethics texts used in contemporary East
Asian schools still emphasize the inseparability of morality and politics and
maintain that duty consciousness is more important than rights consciousness.

GENDER, FAMILY, AND HIERARCHY

The societies of East Asia are all characterized by explicit social hierarchies, subordination of the individual to the family, and subordination of females to males—repressive qualities that emerge from an otherwise humanistic Confucian tradition. Whereas some Western scholars are troubled by the apparent contradiction, Schwartz offered a different view. He commented that "we are all children of the Enlightenment" in the sense that as Westerners we express discomfort with the notion of hierarchy and authority and tend to think that those characteristics should be overcome by reason. He said there is a certain arrogance in denying the role of hierarchy and authority in Asia, considering that those features have not been eliminated from Western societies. He suggested that status and hierarchy may have value that civilizations influenced by Confucianism have more easily accepted.

Henry Rosovsky urged that hierarchy be viewed as a dynamic concept rather than one that is either present or not. Participants considered whether those low in the social hierarchy may seek fulfillment in the proper conduct of their lowly role. It was suggested, for example, that female shop attendants in Japan find a means of self-expression in the elaborate but essentially meaningless task of hand-wrapping packages in the distinctive style dictated by the company for which they work. This raised questions about whether individuals are content with their lot in life or whether the social hierarchy in which each person defines one's role is indeed repressive.

Tu said that since the May Fourth Movement, the hierarchical foundation of the family and society, expressed in terms of three bonds (*sangang;* father–son, husband–wife, and ruler–ruled), is the aspect of the Confucian tradition most criticized. However, these relationships are described in the Confucian literature as the basis of mutual social obligations that guide correct, humane, harmonious relations; they are based on age differentiation, division of labor, or status and have been viewed as defining characteristics of any complex society.

Social hierarchy is also reinforced by the continuity of relations with one's parents long into one's adulthood. Tu said that even today, Asian adults have close, dependent ties to their parents. This is intended as an expression of compassion and respect for those who gave life to, nurtured, and taught one to behave in a civilized fashion, but often it infantilizes an otherwise grown person by subordinating one to parental demands. In Chinese, the written character for adult has a graphic component that implies that adulthood is not only an achieved state but also a developmental process. This outgrowth of

Confucian tradition also generates a widespread veneration of, and deference to, age.

Another byproduct of the Confucian family process of socialization is that one is taught the virtues of self-sacrifice for long-range gratification and discouraged from seeking immediate gains. Endurance, self-control, and the ability to put off for the future are fostered within the family, as is the sense that one must subordinate one's own preferences for the benefit of the family. Lessons one learns about one's role and responsibility in the family have ramifications for the broader social and political contexts.

Females are especially constrained by the hierarchy that emerges from Confucian traditions. Kim Kwang-ok questioned whether there is much respect for females' subordinate role in Korean society. He said a woman is identified first as a mother and has no independent status or private identity apart from that role. Kalton pointed out than the Korean language itself encourages hierarchical thinking. It is impossible to address another person with more than a few words before having to determine the status of one's relationship with that person, because the language is built on a code of hierarchy about mutual relationships.

Two other features of East Asian life that appear to stem from the Confucian emphasis on hierarchy are the division of household space on hierarchical or gender-related grounds and the practice of rote learning. Both seem to pervade life at all economic levels in East Asian societies. Both offer the individual a sense of fitting into a grander, preestablished value system, either spatially temporally. Rote learning, after all, is a concession to past experience and a confirmation of one's significance by the privilege of internalizing the collected wisdom of one's elders and teachers.

POLITICAL CULTURE AND ECONOMIC ETHICS

Tu said that Confucian humanism is associated with an agricultural economy within an authority-based polity. Outside the agricultural society, Confucian values are less prominent and are emphasized as a form of family ethics. This phenomenon raises questions about whether Confucian values are wedded to agricultural economies or whether they may be adapted to industrial econo-mies too. This issue is linked to the question of whether Confucian ethics are compatible with democratization.

Carter Eckert discussed the view of profit in a Western capitalist system on the one hand and in Korea on the other. Although avarice is not valued anywhere, capitalist societies place no moral onus on an individual's pursuit of profit, because through the mechanism of the marketplace, one's own greed stimulates the economy and serves a larger purpose. In Korea, capitalism was imported by the Confucian literati. They resolved the apparent conflict between Confucian attitudes of disapproval regarding the pursuit of individual gain and the profit motive inherent in capitalism by claiming that the central purpose of profit was to improve the general quality of life and ensure the nation's independence. Productivity and development were encouraged by the activities of hero-merchants, who were expected to subordinate their own interests to the nation's.

The participants discussed the economic behavior of other East Asian states. They recognized that one communality in East Asia is the central and active role of the government, which directs the state's economic activity. Differences in the particular role played by the state, however, made it difficult to characterize that role as a reflection of a particular Confucian mentality.

POPULAR THOUGHT AND RELIGION

James Watson said that anthropologists are skeptical about defining behavior observed in peasant culture as Confucian. He said that the extensive clan organizations characteristic of Chinese peasant life are frequently misconstrued as social-welfare systems that reflect the supposedly Confucian emphasis on familial cohesion. He believes that they are instead "hard-nosed business corporations" ruthlessly run by "steely eyed managers" whose primary concern is to restrict benefits to the legitimate descendants of a particular ancestor.

The cult of ancestor worship associated with such practices is commonly seen as an expression of respect for elders, a universalized display of filial piety. Although powerful lineage groups do build elaborate halls to honor their ancestors, these are entirely financed by the ancestors' estates. Once the estate of a deceased relative ceases to provide profit for the living, his descendants forget about him and shift their attention to a more profitable forebear.

Watson said that intellectual historians have been duped by the self-serving rhetoric of Chinese scholar-bureaucrats who perpetuate the myth that such popular practices reflect Confucian ideals. Chinese may attribute their behavior to Confucian tradition even if they are not truly motivated by Confucian concerns, because this enables them to foster the illusion of cultural unity. Watson asserted that one's identity as Chinese emerges from correct, ritual behavior—orthopraxy. One participates in certain communal rites (e.g., marriage, funerals) and even agrees about the meaning of such rituals without necessarily believing the explanation. The key to being Chinese is acceptance of external, ritual form, not adherence to an internal, conceptual orthodoxy.

Schwartz objected to Watson's equation. Considering that the original rituals of the past have been completely forgotten, that there is great uncertainty about the nature and significance of the surviving rituals, and that large subgroups in China are not concerned with orthopraxy, the performance of rituals is an unreliable definition of what it means to be Chinese.

COMPARATIVE PERSPECTIVES

Tu views Confucianism as more than a code of social ethics; it is a religion with a considerable spiritual dimension, but it is unlike other religions. Some religions, such as Buddhism, Christianity, and Islam, have assumed a variety of cultural forms. Others, such as Shinto, are culturally specific and cannot be transplanted beyond their indigenous civilizations. Confucianism is neither.

Confucianism is not a religion limited to a particular culture, race, or nationality. It is a dynamic force that flows, has different currents, and has the capacity to interact with other traditions in a pluralistic context. However, there is no Confucian community that one may join, analogous to a church, shrine, or synagogue. One cannot simply convert to Confucianism and identify oneself as Confucian; one must become Confucian through self-transformation. The driving question is how to find the inner resources for transformation.

Confucius accepted the world as redeemable. He viewed the political realm in moral terms and accepted the power-based hierarchical relations that emerge from the political realm as a resource for transformation. An individual must develop as a moral being within the human relationships that bind one to society, not in an abstract, transcendent state. This optimistic view is predicated on the tragic paradox that although everyone is perfectible through self-effort, one can never realize one's potential for self-transformation to a fully moral being, no matter how hard one tries. Not even Confucius is viewed as the highest example of human perfection. Christ and Sakyamuni are the paradigms of virtue in Christianity and Buddhism, but it is possible to envision one more Confucian, more sagely, than Confucius; he failed to realize his own goals.

Confucianism may be regarded as a language of moral community flowing from a universal moral value. The vital energy inherent in human relationships offers a way to transform society and to establish a particular political structure. For that reason, a dominant theme in Confucian political ideology is ethics not power. In a Confucian state, political order has primacy, and the central government is the locus of power. Throughout East Asia, the state is seen as a mechanism for exerting social control and establishing and maintaining moral order. The state is expected to serve as an exemplar, and even though those who staff it may not be committed to Confucian values, they are entrusted with an obligation and a right to establish moral order. This is often done by moral persuasion as well as by coercive force.

The Confucian state is expected to play a range of roles in citizens' lives. It is expected to educate the populace, to guide social interaction, and to prepare and recruit future state officials. The state's monopoly on access to education enables it to promote a comprehensive vision of society and to prohibit other social groups from developing an independent consciousness different from that promulgated by the state. As a result, Chinese society is infused with Confucian rhetoric, which even permeates the language used by other Chinese religions.

Since the nineteenth century the Confucian world, which contributed so much to the development of China, collapsed as the Chinese were drawn into a highly integrated universe. The rhetoric of wealth and power supplanted the language of morality. Some say that neither the spiritual threat of Buddhism nor the military threat of the Mongols damaged the Confucian world as badly as the West has in the past century and a half.

In the 1960s some social scientists believed that modernization was a universal process and modernity a universal ambition. After the disintegration of the Confucian world and the "beginning" of development, they rejected the traditions of East Asia as irrelevant to the transformation underway. These assumptions turned out to be problematic and have impelled a reexamination of East Asia in terms of the various manifestations of contemporary Confucianism.

Stephen Graubard recalled Shimuel Eisenstadt's criticism of efforts to assess modernization exclusively in quantitative terms and suggested that the preconditions that characterized each society help to explain why modernity takes different forms in different places. Graubard endorsed the importance of exploring ideas that have survived from the Confucian world of the past, however attenuated in form, to influence contemporary East Asia. He suggested that the Weberian approach to the study of Asia be put aside in favor of studying the potential of Confucian ideas, particularly those concerning the role of the state, to influence the world beyond Asia.

Rosovsky defended the Weberian question, saying that it is worth understanding why some states develop more rapidly or more fully than others and what commonalities, if any, are present among East Asian states. Schwartz objected to Weber's attention to economic and technical growth as the prime gauge of development and suggested that greater attention be paid to the influential role of the family.

George De Vos noted Durkheim's view that the main feature of modernization is a change toward secularization. With the emergence of science, human thought about the supernatural was supplanted by a more secular morality. The idea that the mundane is governed by the intentional intervention of supernatural beings was replaced with a rational view of mechanical causality. Religion, then, may be distinguished from secular morality and rational causality by an orientation toward a source of sacredness and a belief in the intentional intervention of the supernatural in the affairs of humanity. De Vos challenged the assertion that Confucianism is a religion and asked whether it is possible to identify what agency determines morality in the Confucian context. He said that in Confucianism, one must look to some source other than the supernatural for the embodiment of the sacred. A system of thought can be considered a religion only if something is held sacred within that system.

In Christianity, the continuity of the tradition emerges from the church and the sense of eternity. In Buddhism, the ego disappears into the cosmos. In Confucianism, the ego disappears into the family; the cult of ancestor worship provides a sense of continuity and may be seen as the seat of the sacred, or religious, element of Confucianism.

Roderick MacFarquhar said that most contemporary East Asians do not share the elite's concern about identity as Chinese or Japanese but do care about what it means to be an individual in a Confucian family. Confucius was right to emphasize the family's role as the root of stability, and it is incumbent on those who wish to understand Confucianism to examine the traditions from the bottom up, not from the top down.

Peter Bol said that China failed to preserve the traditions it originated. In his opinion, some present-day intellectuals, including Tu Weiming, have radically redefined Confucianism as a set of contrived values that do not accurately reflect the traditions. Bol believes that it is important to reexamine the original bases of Confucianism and is appalled that the Confucian classics are no longer a part of the Confucian curriculum. He objects to the manipulation of ideas by the elite to formulate a vision of Chinese society that is ostensibly in accordance with the Confucian tradition yet is devoid of regard for the original sources of values.

Dore added that in Japan, certain magical themes gradually became dissociated from their classical origins. Confucianism, for example, was partially transformed into a set of guiding moral principles divorced from the sanction of any supernatural force; it became entirely secularized.

Tu concluded by saying that the worldview of contemporary Chinese intellectuals has been so altered by Western ideas and the disjunctures of the past century that the Confucian world order is as alien to them as it is to non-Chinese. He said it is not clear that modern Confucian humanism is a reflection of elite mentality or that the best way to understand Confucianism is to take the state as the locus of moral order. The Chinese state is now in the process of disintegration, and its legitimacy, as well as that of the ruling elite, has been undermined. This conference on Confucian institutions made clear the need to look beyond the political arena to the family as the source of moral order and to redefine the cultural elite.

The Problematique of the Confucian Value Orientation

EZRA VOGEL OPENED the workshop by stating that this was the first of a series of four such symposia regarding the rise of industrial East Asia (Japan and the Four Mini-Dragons—South Korea, Taiwan, Hong Kong, and Singapore) which would be convened at the Academy during the next several years. The other three will focus on the influence Japanese development has had on the rest of the world (chaired by Professor Vogel), the influence of Japan and other newly industrialized countries in East Asia on the further development of the PRC (chaired by Roderick MacFarquhar), and lessons the West can learn from Asia's economic development (chaired by Henry Rosovsky).

Tu Weiming, in his role as the chairman of this first conference, said that the format of this meeting was intended to be flexible. He said that Confucian humanism is a common discourse in East Asia, an ongoing conversation involving scholars representing various academic disciplines, who focus on different parts of the East Asian region, and who examine the issues from different levels of analysis. It is a discourse which moves beyond a discussion of the classical literature associated with the Confucian tradition to an understanding of how the values are manifested in the lives of those who inherit the tradition. Consequently, the format would be simple and informal. While no papers were to be presented, certain participants would be called upon to open each session by making brief presentations and then to guide the conversation.

Benjamin Schwartz began by observing that questions regarding the relationship between Chinese culture and modernization have been discussed over such a long period that it is not clear anything new may be said about it. To those who doubt or diminish the significance of culture in the process of modernizing, he joked that the importance should be evident from the interest in convening such a conference.

Schwartz suggested that the Confucian institutions the conference was intended to address may be seen as the shared cultural orientations of East Asia. When we speak of Confucianism do we mean these shared cultural orientations? Is there something called Confucianism that we can all refer to? Schwartz, however, insisted that he will continue to speak of Confucianism (some do not believe we should do so). One reason he does so stems from the *Analects* and Confucius's claim, *shuerbuzuo*, that he is not a creator of ideas but a transmitter, that he is the quintessence of Chinese culture, and that he is just transmitting it. Schwartz challenged this assertion, suggesting that Confucius plays a greater role than he acknowledged by not only transmitting mentalities, but also reflecting on their nature. Schwartz asserts that Confucius raised troubling questions about the nature of the society he observed around him and attempted to discern why social order did not function as it had the potential to, or as it had in the past. He said that Confucius identified certain mentalities that are the essence of Chinese culture, some of which are pre-Confucian, such as the tremendous stress on the family. So Schwartz believes that there is such a thing as Confucianism. Another reason for believing in Confucianism is the presence in China of tendencies that may share cultural assumptions with Confucianism, but that run in quite another direction. Schwartz has come more and more to the view that if China has responded well to modernization, that what is often called Legalism may have something to do with it, just as Confucianism has. Thus there are other conscious reflective tendencies in the high culture aside from Confucianism.

Noting the title of the workshop, Schwartz questioned the notion of Confucian institutions since the relationship down through the centuries of institutions identified with Confucianism was a problematic one. Thus when speaking of an institution he would rather see it as an institution influenced by Confucianism, rather than a Confucian institution. Furthermore, he said he does not believe that institutions have any greater "ontological reality" than, say, the state. Rather institutions may be viewed as the space where norms and ideas interact with material and power interests.

Schwartz noted that when he first entered the field of Chinese studies, one central concern—in keeping with the Weberian hypothesis—was the extent to which Confucianism was an impediment to modernization. Weber questioned whether or not Confucianism serves as the "functional equivalent" of the Protestant work ethic. Schwartz does not believe it does, but also does not abide by the view that the "Confucian ethic" inhibits economic growth or is an obstacle to modernization. He noted that although Talcott Parsons's definition of "achievement" versus "ascription" was widely discussed, it had never occurred to scholars at that time to ask why "achievement" cannot be applied to groups (such as lineages) as well as individuals.

There is currently a tendency to view Confucianism as having been very favorable to modernization in all its aspects. In Schwartz's view, to the extent that Confucianism had its own high cultural ideas, it was not a block to modernization, but it wasn't particularly looking in that direction. Nevertheless, there are many cultural practices associated with Confucianism that, once modernization gets underway, proved to be very favorable to it, such as the habits of industry and collective discipline which Confucianism seems to promote. Schwartz notes that Weber was not only concerned with the initiation of industrialization and its relation to the Protestant ethic, but also with something that had little to do with it: industrial society as a "going concern." In his discussions of a fully rationalized, industrialized economy, he shifts the stress away from the individual entrepreneur to the side of effective bureaucratic organization, hierarchy status and authority, and group discipline. The performance of Japan and the Four Mini-Dragons of East Asia should dispel the notion that "Confucian states" cannot modernize or develop. Schwartz points out the possibilities of social critiques based on Confucianism. For, in his view the highest orientation of Confucian culture was not so much to the idea of limitless economic growth, even though it accepted the role that economics plays in people's lives. Rather its ideal of society very much stressed harmony and peace and economic comfort at a very modest level, since without endless growth there must be a concern with limits and distribution.

Schwartz next turned to the political legacy of Confucianism and its influence on the development of democracy and noted that many people now stress that Confucianism is more than has been described in text books: that it very much stressed individual self-development. While he would tend to agree, especially in the case of Neo-Confucianism, Schwartz, though, notes the need to distinguish between differences in the way "individual" is conceptualized in East Asia and the West. Rather than rights consciousness, it refers to whether an individual has the capacity to improve himself morally, more virtue ethic of Alastair MacIntyre [the author of *After Virtue*] rather than rights ethic. He observed that the political demonstrations that were then erupting in Beijing among the students drew upon tradition because, to the extent that there was a concept of "citizenship" in China, one might say that the citizens were the educated members of society—often the youth—who frequently presumed to bear the burden of responsibility for state policy. This resonates well with the latter Han dynasty and the students at the Taixue (T'ai-hsüeh) and their criticism leveled against the state.

He also questioned the view of Thomas Metzger [author of *Escape from Predicament*] that Zhu Xi and Wang Yangming would be pleased if they were brought back to life and had an opportunity to comment on the four dragons. He hypothesized that Neo-Confucians might have quite a few objections to the way in which those states had developed, especially because of ecological matters and excessive consumerism. Schwartz ended by observing that Confucius would be no happier than Calvin would be to return to life and see what has become of the society he had a stake in spurring to development.

Ezra Vogel introduced Professor Tu Weiming, who, he said, was both an intellectual activist and an active thinker. Tu opened by commenting that the Confucian tradition is rife with paradoxes. He views it more as a restless landscape than a static structure. Beginning with the question, "who is a Confucian?" one can see that the scholar officials are commonly regarded as the bearers of the tradition—the paradigmatic examples of a Confucianism, as "ministers of the political order" (to use Diane Oberchaine's term), transmitters of *ru* *(ju)*. From that perspective, Confucianism is seen as a form of political ideology, very much related to the mentality of the mandarins.

Others, notably Professor Yü Ying-shih at Princeton University, have done considerable work trying to understand Confucians as *zhishi fenzi* intellectuals. The claim has been made by a scholar in China, Pang Pu, that only in the case of China would one be able to write a comprehensive history of the intellectual, from the period of the Warring States to modern times. The term *zhishi fenzi* can be used throughout Chinese history, and we can still identify some core meaning to the term, for example, the Song intellectuals, the Donglin intellectuals, the Qing dynasty intellectuals, and then the May Fourth and post-May Fourth intellectuals. The intellectual here is viewed as a concerned, engaged, and politically relevant person.

But Tu's own work has focused on the Confucian tradition as a spiritual tradition, involving the whole question of self-transformation and predicated on the belief that the self is at the center of relationships and not subsumed by them. While Confucian values have long emphasized the dignity and internal autonomy of the individual, this by conscious choice has never been developed into a doctrine of individualism. This is part of the reason that the emphasis on the dignity of the person does not necessarily provide the Chinese with the symbolic resources needed for developing the theory of human rights. Indeed, William Theodore de Bary speaks of Confucianism as more concerned with "human rites" than with "human rights," or, to use T'ang Chun-i's terminology, duty consciousness rather than rights consciousness.

When looking at society we see the importance of the notion of the family; community, polity, or even states in China can be viewed as the family writ large. There is an overall orientation toward conciliation and harmony and a deep-seated anxiety concerning disorder *(luan)*. Even the Confucian golden rule [do not do to others what you would not have them do to you] is predicated on the notion that order should prevail, that disorder is dangerous, and hence that discipline is necessary.

This leads to the issue of polity. Many people believe the Confucians aspired to maximum government in which the authority of the state penetrates deeply to every level of society to ensure the well-being of the populace, defined in ethical and religious as well as in political and economic terms. Indeed, the government is responsible for education at all levels. The result of this is that the government imposes a certain kind of ideological control, or, in E. P. Thompson's terms, "symbolic control." The government is worried about the total outlook of the person, including even unconscious ideas. A highly politicized Confucian state could be highly repressive.

Tu continued by saying that Confucian humanism is neither secular nor transcendent. It is "anthropocosmic" in that it embraces a concern for both the secular world here and now and the world beyond *(tian)*. It does not aim exclusively to satisfy either human concerns or cosmic ones. It is, as Herbert Fingarette wrote, regarding the secular as sacred, although his portrayal of Confucianism as very much informed by ritual rather than deep-rooted personal conviction is problematic.

Tu concluded by saying these issues are highly complicated and that many of those who dealt primarily with the texts are not particularly sensitive to the behavioral manifestations of Confucian culture at all levels: the merchant class, peasantry, mechanisms of control. Tu noted that upon revisiting China several times since 1978 he has come to the realization that there is another picture that is extremely negative and that he is often reminded of Walter Benjamin's view that some of the greatest ideas or values once intertwined with the structure of power may become very dangerous. The Confucian culture is so pervasive and exists at so many different levels that there are a host of distorted images of the system as well. If the Confucian tradition is not properly addressed, whether one takes a positive or negative view, then an understanding of China, and by implication, the Sinic world, would be incomplete.

Peter Bol said that reflecting on Chinese history for the last millennium, the *problematique* of the Confucian value orientation is to conceive of a unitary basis for integrative and unifying values in such a way as to privilege the elite and its culture. The "tension" in the Confucian value orientation is thus between two approaches to culture. First: some have supposed that there can be a single culture which fully represents unifying values. This can lead to a very rigid culture that is not capable of flexibility and change. Second: some have supposed that unifying values are abstractions that cannot be reduced to fixed cultural forms and have, thus, defended diversity within elite culture as different means of representing universals. The danger here is that the appreciation of cultural diversity will obscure the idea of unity. This tension has been endemic to the intellectual culture of the elite during the last millennium.

The intellectual culture of the last one thousand years has been marked by self-conscious thought about values; at times such thought has been highly abstract. It has also been self-critical; one might even say that the history of Chinese thought is a history of criticism. Finally, an elite intellectual culture has continued to exist, although its content has changed.

But why did an intellectual culture exist? I would start from two facts. The political fact is that political power must maintain a unified social-political order and that the continued existence of a national elite is necessary to this (whether it is identified by an examination system or party membership). The social fact is that the size of the elite far exceeds the number of positions available in formal political institutions.

Out of these facts emerge a tension within the dominant set of elite values (whether it tends to either a rigid culture or cultural diversity). On the one hand, political unity must be defended, for without it there would be no institutional defenses of elite privilege. On the other hand, independence from political power and intellectual autonomy must be defended, for without them the dispensation of elite status would be left in the hands of those in government.

The role of intellectual culture is to accomplish both aims at once. That is, to inculcate the idea of unity and unifying values (in the interest of political unity) while at the same time to demonstrate that the dominant form of learning and education at the time is a way of realizing those same values irrespective of whether one holds office or not (in the interest of the social elite). Still, the dilemma remains: what kind of culture is necessary to realize those values. It is typical of the orthodoxies of the last millennium (including Maoism) to claim that while true values are indeed universal only participants in elite culture can realize them, an attitude that has led to a certain cultural rigidity and ossification. Against these orthodoxies there has always been a more liberal view in which, typically, it is held that while there is a single foundation for values it should be apprehended and translated into social guides in diverse ways.

The problem with the Confucian *problematique* so construed is this is: can the *problematique* itself exist if the elite no longer believe that there are universal values or that there is no real basis for such values. One might even ask if there can continue to be a China without such an elite belief. In the modern search for elite values I doubt that "wealth and power" *(fuqiang)* can fill the bill (it has been tried before). First, it fails to satisfy the demand for moral means and, second (more important perhaps), it has traditionally (and recently), meant an increase in state wealth and power at the expense of private interests, and thus directly threatened the elite's ability to maintain the sources of wealth and power it needs to survive. I doubt that the "West" can serve as a unifying source of elite values, at least in the long run, since further exploration will reveal soon enough the internal dissonance of our culture. The question may well be whether a credible case can be made for "Confucian humanism."

Discussion

The discussion focused on the issue of whether wealth and power had ever in fact served as the unifying values of the Chinese system.

Roderick MacFarquhar said, in response to Peter Bol's comments, that the assertion that wealth and power were not sufficient to unify the state because they would elevate the state at the expense of the individual was not necessarily the case. In fact, it can be shown that private individuals can make enormous contributions. Hence this belief by the Chinese was a mistake.

Chang Hao asked Bol whether wealth and power were indeed a major goal for China during the past millennium. Bol said that was occasionally the goal, but that the elite turned away from it in the traditional premodern past because wealth and power increased the power of the state and took no heed of the morality of means.

Richard Madsen observed that it may not have been a turning away from wealth and power per se, but rather from unlimited wealth and power. Was it not fair to say that Confucians were quite happy to have money and power, but with a sense that there should somehow be constraints?

Ronald Dore asked Bol how he would fit in the traditional doctrines about the duties of ruler in agrarian societies in which there is a recurring theme that if you exact too much from the peasants they will not grow crops properly, thereby leading to a diminution in the wealth of the state and the power of the ruler, and that the cycles of history are largely a consequence of people forgetting how to run agrarian societies. Secondly, the bulk of traditional statecraft writings seem to envisage a rather static technology and economy, with no notion of ever-increasing wealth as the result of ever-increasing improvement in technology or government. Were there before the nineteenth century any signs of growth economics within the Confucian tradition?

Bol responded to the first question by noting that these issues had been well represented by debates in the eleventh century between Sima Guang and Wang Anshi. Sima Guang explicitly articulated the fear that if a state starts to take too much then it ultimately hurts the system and destroys itself. Production, held Sima Guang, cannot be expanded beyond population. Wang held for the opposite position in defending his "New Policies" that, in fact, the state's increase in its wealth and power is not at the expense of private interests; there can be a general increase in production, and "managing wealth can create wealth" *(licai jiushi shengcai)*.

Schwartz brought up the role of Legalism. One reason for not calling the Chinese state just Confucian is that the cast of attitudes which came to be called Legalism in ancient China continued to influence the state down through the centuries, even when the name was not explicitly used. There was a perception in pre-unification China that there was a clear relation between production and the power of the state. Schwartz would tend to agree with Creel, who sees in this period an anticipation of the notion of the rationalization of society for state goals. Two forms of Legalism existed. One embodied a physiocratic outlook; it saw agriculture as the only form of wealth. By the time of the Han dynasty we find another variety which stresses mercantile activities under government control and even speaks of foreign trade. The *Han Discourses on Iron and Salt (Yantielun)* provide a classical exposition of this view. This discussion continued throughout history into the modern period of East Asia. In Japan, one of the defiant slogans of the Meiji Restoration was *fukoku kyohei* ("enrich the nation, strengthen the military"). This did not preclude, as was also the case with the Chinese thinker Yan Fu, the notion that actually the ultimate goal should be a private economy. For them, the example of England proved that, in order to gain great power, the only way to have economic development was through a private economy, albeit with a different perspective on what a private economy is. This is reminiscent of Weber's description of the Mercantilist period in the West's development, which witnessed conflict among the states, governments which were not necessarily antimercantile, and a technology which stressed military rationalization. Hence, it may well be that the Mercantilist period helped lay the foundation for economic development in the West. Perhaps a new variety of economic history is needed in the West, one that does not just discuss the romance of the individual entrepreneur, but one that also addresses the question of the development of the infrastructures which could be very easily put under this heading of *fukoku kyohei*.

Rozman observed that the comments of Bol and Schwartz reveal an interesting contrast between China and Japan. On the one hand, in China there was a large elite with no posts, while in Japan, there was an ethic which emerged quickly of making the state richer and stronger. Are the two related? Is the fact that the Chinese elite are not in positions of control a source of weak state Confucianism, not emphasizing the state's role? Whereas in Japan, the fact that the samurai, who were the major bearers of the Confucian tradition, were dependent on state stipends increases the emphasis on the need for a strong state.

Wang Gungwu added that, if one looks at the large Dutch and British companies active in East Asia in the nineteenth century, or for that matter the Portuguese and Spanish before them, one finds that many of the commercial activities were state sponsored, in contrast to the Chinese, who were working against the interests of the state. From the Chinese perspective, the origins of the successors to the mercantilist state in Asia are to be found in the ways of these European national enterprises. An early Chinese understanding of how economic development had been achieved in the West was that it was not private, but state-sponsored. Perhaps this is what influenced the Meiji reformers.

Peter Berger posed the question of exactly what the problem referred to in the title of the session really was. Different people are talking about very different problems. Is the problem the role of Confucian values in the history of China for the last thousand years? In different East Asian countries? Some internal problems of the Confucian worldview? Or, as had been expected, the role of Confucian values *today?* Some clarification as to the problem to be focused on would be useful.

Tu Weiming responded that the *problematique* of the Confucian orientation is first of all internal. We need, for example, to distinguish Confucianism of the elite culture versus that of the popular culture; Confucianism of its original formulation versus its more vulgarized manifestations. At the same time, there is also the fascinating issue of how this value orientation interacts with conceptions of the self, with the social role, with political organization, even with worldview. While these issues may be divergent, still it seems possible to come to terms with some very basic assumptions about the Confucian orientation and whether there are points of convergence or not. In short, the *problematique* is both internal, in the sense of the conflicts and tensions of perceiving the Confucian tradition by Confucians, people working in the historical field, and specialists in different regions, and at the same time to see whether people working at different levels may come to speak of a complex, common entity, rather than a number of separate ones.

George De Vos said that implicit in the concept of state in the West was the notion of competition. Confucian values, by contrast, are based on a stable society, with an agricultural base, and many of the values seem less based on competition than harmony. Oddly, in the modern era, there seems to be an effort to view Confucian values in a competitive manner by asking how the Confucian world is doing vis-à-vis the West and why it is doing so well comparatively. The concept of competition versus the West and how it fits into the value structure of Confucianism needs to be discussed. This manner of viewing Confucianism is a modern invention. The Japanese had to enter into a competitive concept of their well-being: they were being attacked by the West and they responded to it. They armed themselves, went into China, and even gained the same benefits in China as the Western nations. The Japanese concept of themselves and where they were going was in a competitive world. Chinese Confucianism, on the other hand, as a national polity did not have a concept of competition, yet individual Confucian families went out and did well competitively in the outer world. On one level, Confucianism is a concept of government, while on another level it is a concept of adaptation of a family going out into a world that is different.

Roderick MacFarquhar questioned whether De Vos's assertion regarding the competitive aspects of Japanese expansion said more about Confucian competitiveness or Japanese competitiveness. He pointed out that while the Japanese may have felt compelled to model their foreign behavior after the West following their opening to the outside, the Chinese were also exposed to the outside world and did not choose the same approach. If one were to assert that the competitive aspect of Confucian values accounts for the Japanese expansion, one would then need to account for China's failure to develop in the same way.

Bol, too, said that he was uncomfortable with the notion that competition is foreign to the Chinese tradition. While competition for profit was considered dangerous, at the same time there were institutions that were extremely competitive, such as the entire examination system. The argument against competition was that ways had to be found to restrain it rather than eliminating it. As to why China did not respond to the West in the same manner as Japan, Bol speculated that one reason is that China is so large that the flow of resources to the center is so great that people at the center are reluctant to concern themselves with disturbing that order. Much is to be gained, rather, by trying to hold the old order together.

Offering clarification about the Meiji Restoration and how Japan differed from China, Samuel Yamashita noted that the Meiji ruling class primarily consisted of warriors who had a profound understanding of power; the biographies of major figures such as Fukuzawa Yukichi are filled with metaphors of power. There is a good possibility that the Japanese elite were viewing the West in terms of power conflicts. He also noted that the early Meiji intellectuals with Confucian training drew on sets of categories that are oppositional. Thus we find Nishi Yamane invoking the *Book of Changes* and attempting to use imagery from it to explain social Darwinism. At a very deep level these were the only conflictual notions at hand. Also, concerning theories

of growth, there was a period in the early eighteenth century when certain
Japanese Confucian thinkers struggled with economic growth and attempted
to come up with justifications for profit. Among them were, for example,
disciples of Ogyu Sorai, particularly Dasai Shundai. The latter justifies economic profit on two levels. On a metaphysical level, he portrayed commercial
circulation as a natural phenomenon and, hence, entirely appropriate. The
major problem is to control the circulation of goods to prevent its getting out
of hand. The second level is an ethical one. Dasai argued that the desire for
profit is a natural emotion; one need only look to see its ubiquitous nature.
Here, too, the problem is to control the urge to acquire, to become rich. This
is part of a larger transformation of Confucian ethics that began in the late
seventeenth century and ran into the eighteenth century: introspective ethical
doctrines were replaced by others somewhat more outward-looking and more
affirmative of desire.

Chang Hao pointed out (picking up on Dore's questions and remarks by
Schwartz) that Confucian values of the last millennium should not be seen to
have blocked modernization because the statecraft *jingshi* tradition itself
emphasizes growth, albeit not limitless growth. On the other hand, one finds
in the Confucian tradition many things that have nothing to do with modernization. Hence, the Confucian tradition should not be seen merely in terms of
the symbolic resources it contributes to modernization; we should also look in
it for intellectual resources that speak to the issues generated in the process (or
crisis) of modernization.

Schwartz noted that the contrast between China and Japan was viewed in
the past as quite stark. He said that when he first entered the field, the emphasis
was on how much difference there was between the two states, on their
respective *tokushitsu* ("unique character"). Perhaps those differences are there;
certainly Japan always had a sense of its being another state separate from
China, which may have lent itself to a protonationalism of the warrior class.
But, in the end, when China did begin to react to the external situation, one
is struck by how much similarity there is in ways of reasoning. Concerning the
role of profit, already in the work of Mencius we find a recognition of the
legitimate place of merchants in society (albeit at a lower social standing than
the scholarly *shi* class). The antimercantilism of Confucianism has been greatly
overemphasized. Indeed in the *Discourses on Iron and Salt* the Confucians
actively *defend* private merchants and the private economy, within a premodern
capitalistic framework. Many of the attitudes of Yan Fu (about whom Schwartz
wrote a book, *In Search of Wealth and Power*) were similar to those of Fukuzawa,
even though it is unlikely that Yan Fu knew him. With the emergence of the
other so-called dragons, while recognizing the *tokushitsu* of Japan, one tends

to see how much more there is an East Asian world culture. Just as in the West we talk about "Western civilization" and yet go on endlessly about the differences between, say, France and Belgium, or England and Germany, so, too, we have overdone discussions of the differences among the East Asian nations.

Stephen Graubard returned to the questions asked earlier by Berger, which he viewed as fundamental. He noted that the Weberian paradigm was almost immediately challenged by certain Catholic historians. Among their criticisms was the charge that Weber had not dealt with the fact that the social behavior he had described as deriving from Puritanism actually was presented in certain parts of the world that remained positively Catholic. Weber has also been challenged by medievalists such as Jacques Le Goff who charge that he has misrepresented the nature of medieval society, and therefore that the whole question of the importance of Protestantism has been exaggerated. It is also being challenged by scholars such as John Brewer (author of *The Sinews of Power: War and the English State, 1688–1783*), who questions not the importance of the capitalist class or the merchant class, but rather the importance of the state. Thus, Britain, a weak state in the seventeenth century, suddenly became capable of defeating Louis XIV, the Dutch, Louis XV, and so on, losing only one major war in the whole eighteenth century. The role of the state is accorded the greatest importance in explaining this. Turning to the matters at hand, what, then, is the principal interest of the workshop? Is it the fact that a certain part of the world which was previously inconspicuous for its industrial development has become very conspicuous for it in the last forty years? Should we not also be interested in similar phenomena elsewhere, such as the Mediterranean region?

Wang Gungwu remarked that the Confucian tradition is often thought of synonymously with the Chinese tradition. As Graubard noted, the role of the state is important. For example, on the matter of competition, what really created a problem for the Chinese was that they had created an elaborate tributary system in which there was no competition, at least by their own values. Any such competition was viewed as outside, as barbarian matters which did not affect the Chinese. Out of their agrarian value orientations they constructed a very elaborate scheme of the world order. When the West came, they viewed it as peripheral to an intact, integrated, and very rational tributary system, which was able to cope with the strains right up to the nineteenth century. It did very well for China for almost one thousand years. Agreeing with Schwartz, Wang said that he does not believe that Confucianism, in itself, stands in the way of merchants or competition for profit among merchants, within limits—as long as the state is not threatened. As the *Discourses on Iron and Salt* shows, it is fine to make money, as long as it is not too much. Due respect must be paid by the merchants to the state and to the mandarins who guard the interests of the imperial state. Wang's most recent work is on the Chinese in Southeast Asia. They are of interest because they were the first Chinese to live for centuries outside the literati system. For the first time, there was the possibility of sustained commercial efforts without the possibility of the literati or mandarins interfering with their trade. In the official Chinese view, in fact, they were outlaws who had gone beyond the pale of civilization. There they were no longer dependent on the mandarins as they were in China, where, for example, one branch of a clan would become literati, while another (lesser) branch would become merchants. The Chinese of Southeast Asia, however, were forced to adopt other strategies. Once they were outside the literati system, the Chinese discovered that local leaders did not make the same demands on them as the mandarinate at home. The Chinese dealt with the Spanish, Portuguese, Thai kings, and Malaccan rulers. They discovered that they could operate with others who shared merchant values, and so they worked out new rules which ultimately gave rise to capitalism. This illustrates how the state in China embodies the values of the mandarinate and how a value system can be transformed into a tool of the Chinese state. The *problematique* of Confucian values, then, is how does the system get hijacked by the state for its own purposes?

MacFarquhar addressed the question of the *problematique* of the workshop raised by Graubard. We see in the East the acceptance of certain techniques and values that had hitherto prevailed only in the West and the use of these values and techniques to such an extent that the West is challenged for the first time since the Industrial Revolution. The *problematique* then is how to account for this enormous phenomenon in East Asia. A task for a later conference will be the issue of why it is that in the land of its formation Confucianism has been so singularly unsuccessful, if indeed it is Confucianism that has promoted economic development. MacFarquhar's way of explaining this is that the merchants of Southeast Asia are members of that commercial, coastal class who have been liberated from the dead hand of northern bureaucracy. An interesting feature of the economic development in East Asia, compared to Europe, is that it is the periphery which has been successful, if we take China as the center of Confucian culture. In the case of Europe, it was in the major countries of Western Europe that industrialism developed and from which it spread out to the periphery. Also, MacFarquhar believes that it is the "bourgeois Confucian" values of the coastal merchants that are critical to economic development and not the elite state values, which indeed may well be, as Schwartz pointed out, more legalist and Confucian. Confucianism is not, supposedly, a doctrine for a strong, centralized state. The Confucian values of interest to us are at the level of the family—those that promote competition, commercial competition, which have been so successful outside China and may be well be allowed in China, as well, in the future. This has already happened in Taiwan.

Carter Eckert closed the session by sharing his thoughts on the matter of values. He asked whether or not there is a connection between values and culture and modernization. He suggested that there are other factors that may also be of importance and wondered how significant the issue of values is. For example, in the case of Japan, the fact that the samurai were not a landed aristocracy seems more important to explaining development there than Confucian values. Korea, on the other hand, had a very entrenched landed aristocracy, which militated against rapid industrialization. He urged that some thought be given to the matter of where values and culture fit on the list of priorities of concerns. Regarding Confucian values specifically, he sought to distinguish between original values, in the texts themselves, and the unintentional values that emerged from the Confucian system, for example, the emphasis on education in a very general sense rather than the emphasis on specific values in writings by Confucius and Mencius. Finally, is not the timing of the industrialization in the respective countries important (as in Dore's work)? In a late-developing context, it would seem, Eckert believes, more important to have a collectivist ethic than in, say, England in the eighteenth century.

Confucian Ethics as a Common Discourse

MICHAEL KALTON BEGAN the second session by setting forth his notion of Confucian ethics as a common discourse. First, he noted that he would consider the issue in its contemporary form and not the earlier manifestations of the Confucian tradition in Korea, although there was clearly much that could said of them as well. Second, he took "discourse" in a somewhat broader sense than "conversation" in its literal sense. Confucian ethics and a Confucian mentality are certainly continuing in Korea, not necessarily on the level of explicit conversation, but on another level. His notion of "discourse" draws upon notions of Peter Berger in the sense of asking what the "conversation of social activity" is and what assumptions are effective in that activity that continue and manifest this mentality.

The Confucian mentality is not found in a pure form in Korea except in a few commonly observable areas such as the ceremonies in honor of Confucius, rites of ancestor veneration, and talk of filial piety, which are found more in the countryside than the city. Kalton would rather look at the overlay of mentalities, how modern and Confucian mentalities fit together. JaHyun Kim Haboush's work on the Korean monarchy in the Choson dynasty, *A Heritage of Kings,* provides a striking description of Confucian mentality in Korea. At the start of the book she notes:

> One of the key understandings of the Confucian worldview is the perception that heaven is rational, that the universe is moral, that human reason is a sufficient instrument to fathom the divine, that man can reproduce on earth the moral order immanent in the universe.

Kalton noted that this view closely parallels what he teaches beginning students trying to understand the development of the modern Western mind out of its roots in the Enlightenment. The categories he uses to describe the Western mentality are: (1) man is rational; (2) nature is like a vast machine operating on causal principles; (3) by mathematics and experiment man can understand nature; (4) man can use scientific reason to control nature and bring about the good life on earth. The two mentalities interact point for point in a very interesting way; there are areas of Korean practice where both are at work, sometimes in creative interaction, sometimes in tension. These points provide a useful framework to understand the interaction.

"Heaven is rational" compared to the proposition "man is rational." "Rational" in these two cases means something quite different. In the Confucian case, this proposition is another way of saying that heaven or the ultimate order of the universe is an order of human relationships, manifested particularly in a hierarchical order. The Western proposition has to do with our power of thinking about things and confidence in this power. Put these two together we have the notion of modern rationality operating in a society where human relationships continue to have a very central role. Thus in the West we focus on a rational, linear argument; but in Korea one would not pursue such an argument without taking into account the question of with whom one is arguing! One might also view this pair as hierarchy versus rational functionalism. Thus a business might be organized in terms of a hierarchy of functions, but if one organizes it both hierarchically *and* functionally, then the result is totally different.

"The universe is moral" versus "nature is a vast machine." The notion of machines emphasizes the objective, the manipulative, the human control aspects of life, and it has entered strongly into the Korean mentality. At the same time, a conviction of the ultimate morality of the universe is still alive. How do these work together? This pair has a particular focus in the political arena, where Korea has a strong tradition of moral discourse as the core of power broking. Traditionally this was between the king and the bureaucracy where the monarch was *primus inter pares,* so that there was a frequent dialogue conducted often in moral terms, thereby frequently engendering problems.

"Human reason can fathom the divine" versus "by math and experiment we can understand nature." This pair is of interest, since along with objective, scientific inquiry comes the project of Confucian cultivation: what are you becoming? And what does the kind of man you are have to do with the kind of thing you say? Kalton noted that he had not found any straightforward combination of these two in Korea. It is not true, in his view, to say that Korea has creatively synthesized moral subjectivity with the kind of objective rationality that focuses on obtaining results. But he has found that there is powerful ongoing concern with self-cultivation that appears in many unexpected areas. For example, with Korean colleagues, informal discussions late into the evening invariably lead to questions of "What techniques do you use for cultivation?

What are your spiritual practices?" This is not an experience readily obtained in the United States!

*"Man can produce on earth the moral order in the universe" versus "man can use scientific reason to control nature and bring about a good life on earth. "*This is the category of motivation; it produces interesting combinations, particularly under the mediation of nationalism. While in the past Confucianism played the role of social unifier in Korean society, nationalism has now largely replaced it. Under such conditions, the seeking after materialistic profit has been turned into a moral duty that you perform in the name of the nation—a moral imperative to go out and make money. Although this fusion of motivations may seem naive to some, it has actually worked to the extent that the Korean government has been invested with the authority to intervene and dictate who is going to make money, how much, and by what kind of arrangements, in ways that would likely outrage Westerners with a capitalist mentality.

Finally, Kalton noted that both these mentalities focus, in the end, on life on earth in the human community; it is therefore possible to bring them together. Unlike the case in the West, where Enlightenment thought acted to displace religion, Confucian thought has not been supplanted through the influence of Western secularism. Accordingly, the kind of society that results from the merging of these mentalities is totally unlike Western secular society, for the overall vision in East Asia of moral meaning in the universe and the way people interrelate has been transformed and not destroyed.

Samuel Yamashita spoke about Confucian ethical discourse as a meta-language, addressing fundamental questions as to the existence and nature of such discourse in Japan. His model of discourse is derived from Foucault: Confucian ethical discourse is seen as having coherence, as being based on certain fundamental oppositions, as bound by certain rules, as operating under certain conditions, but also susceptible to modification. The issue of power, however, is not dealt with here, due to limitations of time.

Yamashita focused on four key elements of this discourse. First is the conception of a moral order, which can be political, economic, or social. The second major conception, derived from Tu Weiming, is self-cultivation, which is seen as the chief means for individuals to realize this moral order and their place in it. Third is the conception of centrality, a sense of a center and a periphery, geographically, symbolically, and morally. Fourth, he argues, is an unmistakable archaism, a valorization of the past, a commitment to the past. However, it is not absolute. Rather it is always the past in tension with the contemporary. There seems to be oscillation along a spectrum that includes the past at one end and the present at the other.

In the case of Japan, one finds evidence of the Confucian ethical discourse in the very earliest extant histories, that is, the *Kojiki* (A.D. 712) and the *Nihon shoki* (A.D. 720). This is hardly surprising, given that they were modeled on Chinese histories; one may find evidence of the historiographic influence of Sima Qian (Ssu-ma Ch'ien) in some of the terminology. These works were commissioned by the newly emerged Yamato clan, which was eager to establish itself as the main ruling family. They saw the histories as a way of legitimizing the Chinese-style state they were creating in the seventh and eighth centuries.

In the *Kojiki* and the *Nihon shoki* one finds a number of elements common to the Confucian ethical discourse. There is, for example, the interest in order, order as privileged. The Yamato clan is presented as Confucian, as moral defenders of the order. Second, one finds that archaism also is privileged. The Yamato are given a past with divine origins. Third, centrality also is featured. The native province of the Yamato is presented as the center; their relatives and allies are elevated over their peers. It is interesting to note that self-cultivation is deemphasized. While one may argue that it is implicit in the characterization of the Yamato rulers as moral rulers, still it is not presented explicitly. One possible explanation for this absence is that it may have been seen as threatening, as a way of encouraging others to empower themselves and present themselves as claimants to power.

The states that commissioned these histories and that would continue to commission similar histories, the Nara and Heian states (710–1185), were the first of a number of states in Japan that invoked Confucian ethical discourse to legitimize their rule. One might even argue that the medieval states implicitly invoked and affirmed this discourse to the extent that authority was seen as deriving from the emperor.

It is in the Tokugawa period (1600–1867) that one sees the fullest flowering of Confucian ethical discourse. Apart from the state's interest in legitimizing itself, there was, for the first time, great interest in self-cultivation. This was in part due to the introduction of new ethical doctrines from Korea and China. These new doctrines inspired new, distinct communities of Confucian discourse, schools in some cases, movements in other. Yamashita would argue that from about 1650 to 1750 the major disputes and debates focused on the issue of self-cultivation; this was a major change from the earlier situation. For example, the school of Yamasaki Anzai focused on spiritual cultivation, while the Hayashi and Bokumon schools concentrated on encyclopedic learning as a form of cultivation. There was the O Yo-mei (Wang Yang-ming) movement, based on a more active notion of self-realization. Also there was the Ancient Learning movement centered on Ito Jinsai and Ogyu Sorai, who turned to Mencius and Xun Zi for guidance in self-cultivation.

The Tokugawa period also presents evidence of the archaizing theme. There was great interest in the Chinese past, in uncovering the "lost" meaning of canonical Confucian texts. Volumes and volumes of commentaries on the Chinese classics were written by Tokugawa Confucians, further evidence of the commitment to archaism.

The centrality of China was also widely accepted by Tokugawa Confucian scholars, as was the marginality of Japan. This is a somewhat complicated issue since the Japanese were never comfortable existing within the Chinese tributary system. They were involved with it only for short periods, and when Korean missions came to Japan in the early Tokugawa period there were enormous diplomatic and ceremonial complications stemming from their different views of the tributary system and their relationship to China. One begins to find a very curious and profound change occurring in the way centrality was handled. Ogyu Sorai, for example, accepted the centrality of classical China, but argued that Tokugawa Japan was somehow closer to classical China than Qing China (1644–1911), that it was the Japanese and not the corrupt Manchu rulers who were approximating the Zhou vision. Ogyu Sorai even saw himself as the direct successor to Mencius and argued that heaven's intervention had allowed him to recover the transmission lost after Mencius and present it to the world.

This period also saw the appropriation of the elements of this Confucian ethical discourse by non-Confucian scholars; an understanding of this development is crucial for understanding this discourse in modern times. A number of groups of such scholars could be mentioned, but the focus here was on perhaps the most important of them, the "Scholars of National Learning" (kokugakusha). They accepted the new philology and the archaistic theme, but substituted a Japanese past for a Chinese one, while structurally using the rhetoric of the Confucian ethical discourse. They also accepted the notion of a Chinese centrality, but replaced China with Japan. This was a very interesting and important term in the history of this concept in Japan.

The other major development in the Tokugawa period was that the Confucian ethical discourse came to have broader currency. One can argue that as a result of the spread of literacy following the development of a publishing industry, and the proliferation of Confucian academies and so-called temple schools that Professor Dore has written about, this ethical discourse spread into the warrior class, the merchant class, and the upper stratum of the peasant class. Not surprisingly, in a number of peasant protests that occurred late in the Tokugawa period one find peasants appealing in the name of Confucian virtues to their local lords in arguing for redress within the terms of the Confucian ethical discourse.

In the modern period, that is, from the Meiji Restoration (1868) on, we find a number of developments of which two will be discussed here. First, one finds that the appropriation of elements of the Confucian ethical discourse by non-Confucians continues. In this case, it is corporate entities that seem to be doing the appropriating: the state and companies. The other major development is that these appropriated, and often revised, elements of Confucian thought reached the population at large for the first time. One might argue that the routes for such transmission were the educational system, military and paramilitary organizations, companies, and the media.

In the 1880s two very important documents were issued by the Meiji state: the 1880 Imperial Rescript to Soldiers and Sailors and the 1890 Imperial Rescript on Education. In both, Confucian ethical rhetoric figures prominently; loyalty and filial piety to the emperor are highlighted.

Early in the twentieth century, the family was revived as the important model for social organization. Many large companies responded to labor unrest by creating company philosophies that used familism. During the 1930s and through World War II a number of elements of the Confucian ethical discourse found their way into state-sponsored ideologies: loyalty, filial piety, harmony, familism. These emerged in obviously modified form, focused on the emperor, on Japanese centrality, and a kind of Japanese archaism.

During the postwar period, the issue of "moral education" (*shushin,* lit. "self-cultivation") surfaced almost as soon as the occupation ended and continued throughout the 1950s, and apparently is still a live issue. In some schools in Japan it is reported that the teachers still read the Imperial Rescript on Education to students.

In conclusion, Yamashita views what has happened in the modern period as an appropriation of the Confucian ethical discourse by corporate entities and by those who claim to speak for corporate entities. Also, for the first time, the population at large became involved in the discourse. Finally, this appropriation is being used primarily to guide, regulate, and even control the population in happy and unhappy ways.

Richard Madsen viewed the contemporary Chinese discourse about Confucian ethics as linked to the international discourse. He discussed the six-part television series, *He shang (River elegy),* which stirred up great intellectual and popular debate when it was broadcast in China in the spring and summer of 1988. The theme of the series is that China's civilization, symbolized by the Yellow River, is in an inexorable decline and there is a desperate need for China to cast off the burdens of its traditions and open itself, like the river, to the Blue Sea (symbolic of the commerce and the science and technology of the Western world).

Madsen commented that while many Westerners who study development and China see it as unwise to completely renounce tradition, the Chinese intelligentsia itself is split about this matter. Some argue that those who advocate the preservation of Chinese cultural traditions (and Tu Weiming is identified as a chief proponent of this) stand from afar beyond the glare of the problems caused by the traditions and hope to restrain China's development by keeping it a quaint and backward place.

Madsen was struck by how caught up the intelligentsia was in China with its role as social critics, drawing on a well-spring of iconoclastic idealism about the need for the renewal of society. There was a coherence to the intellectuals' criticisms of their society which seemed to draw on Confucian ethics. This, Madsen felt, was a reflection of their having been wedded to a long tradition, a common background that served as a foundation for their criticism. Madsen sensed a profound anguish among the intellectuals in the way they used the language of the past to debate the future.

Madsen views the central dilemma as the conflict between Confucian ethics, on the one hand, and the discourse on wealth and power, on the other. In Asia, the two discourses are closely intertwined. In China, the questions are how to make the country wealthier and stronger, which models to choose to make the state flourish as in Taiwan, South Korea, and Japan. This involves a concern that the dynamics of a system that promotes wealth will destroy the social order. Many feel that the modern manifestations of Confucian values which are based on familial values are threatened by modern industrialized civilization because modernization perverts tradition, turning respect for education into an exam-ination hell, for example, and equality of the sexes into the economic exploi-tation of women.

There is a fear that while modernity and development may bring wealth and power, it will also pervert the social order. In the recent past, the marriage of feudal culture and Leninism brought out the worst of Chinese traditions in the form of perversion and destruction of Confucian values. Madsen said that all cultures face these problems and that in the West the family is threatened, too. It is difficult to speak of it cross-culturally because the language of wealth and power has been universalized. Economics has become an international language which is easy to teach people. The existence of such a common mode of discourse influences the way in which we converse and makes it easier for us to speak about these issues than about ethical issues. Ethics involves a holistic way of thinking that requires an enormous amount of humanistic learning, which our universities do not promote because society does not value that.

Ezra Vogel noted that many intellectuals in Japan (and to a lesser extent, perhaps, in Hong Kong and Taiwan) are pleased with what they view as Japan's success and that they probably would not share the sense of anguish felt by the

Chinese. To be sure, there are intellectuals there who raise critical questions concerning the dangers of the drive for wealth and power, but existentially this is a very different situation from China.

Roderick MacFarquhar asked Thomas Gold about how intellectuals in Taiwan would respond to the writers of *He shang*. Would they not tell them that while the PRC has set about destroying traditional culture, they in Taiwan have regarded themselves as the protectors of culture? And that the problem of the PRC is that it had destroyed the wrong part while Taiwan protected the right part?

Gold responded that this is indeed the official Taiwan view. They see the Chinese tradition as very vast, very diverse, and the PRC has emphasized authoritarianism, the state, and not the strength of the family.

Chang Hao responded to this comment by pointing out that there are many diverse opinions held by intellectuals in Taiwan, distinct from the official line. In fact, even in Taiwan the *He shang* mentality is quite widespread, as is evident in the fact that two of the most popular writers now are Bo Yang and Li Ao, who have each written iconoclastic critiques of Chinese culture in the spirit of *He shang*.

Peter Berger said that he would like to introduce an empirically disturbing fact into the conversation, namely, that there is a massive growth of fundamentalist Protestantism in the world today. This phenomenon is especially noticeable in Latin America and Africa, but it is also important in East Asia, most dramatically in South Korea, but also in China. The increasing appeal of a relatively unsophisticated Western religion in East Asia suggests that the common moral discourse which is the subject of the conference has failed to meet the needs of the people who have presumably inherited it. Suddenly, the most Western—and most unsophisticated Western—religious ideology is penetrating the region. How to account for this?

Madsen noted that in the PRC Protestantism is seen as modern and an alternative in a devastated cultural landscape. As a movement it is growing rapidly. Before 1949 there were about one million Protestants in China. Now there may be five or six million.

Kalton added that in Korea, while there has been a massive growth in Protestantism, the rate of growth of the Roman Catholic church has outstripped that of the Protestant church. He speculated that one reason for this appeal might be the importance of ritual in Korean culture, and that the rituals of the Catholic church thus proved deeply satisfying. A second reason might be the deep Catholic concern with authority and orthodoxy. Church membership has also fostered networks of apparently secular associations such as a society of Roman Catholic bankers. The Protestants, however, are those most vocal in opposition to human rights abuses, which the Confucian tradition seems largely to overlook. Indeed, the Confucian tradition is often seen to support exploitation because of its rigorous attention to hierarchical order and sophisticated notions of group mentality. Consequently, there are segments of the society which remain voiceless, as in the case of young female workers in Korea.

Two problems about the presence of Christianity in Korea were posed by Kim Hyung-gyun. He asked how Confucian ethics will survive when both the Protestant and Catholic churches have introduced the concept of transcendence into Korean society. He also wondered how Confucianism in Korea will be transmitted to the next generation in the absence of institutions to perform this.

Benjamin Schwartz objected to the simplistic view of many Asians about the West (largely seen in terms of wealth and power). He said that while they saw the complexities and crises of their own societies, many who romanticize about the West have not fully considered the pre-Enlightenment West or the consequences of the Enlightenment. There is also a tendency to deemphasize or ignore doctrinal differences that are the bases of conflict between different Western thinkers.

Lin Tongqi said that the so-called *He shang* mentality as discussed today can be misleading. The popularity of its iconoclastic message might be exaggerated. One of the reasons why the television serial enjoyed such popularity has less to do with its iconoclastic message than with its mode of presentation. The artistic form *He shang* uses to put such broad and complicated themes on the screen was something completely novel and exciting to the Chinese viewers. Another reason for its success is the veiled political attack it leveled against the Chinese authorities. It demonstrates the real emergence among the Chinese intellectuals of a broad but invisible political united front, which manifested itself in the students' demonstration in Beijing. To support his arguments, Lin said that of the six scholars who were invited in the film to comment, at least four do not endorse the totalistic rejection of traditional values, aesthetic or moral. But they were willing to relinquish their academic positions in a joint political effort to demand a genuine (not mock) democracy, a fully (not partially) open door, and better working and living conditions. A third source of its strong impact is the echo it manages to find of a deeply rooted moral sense largely derived from Confucianism and shared traditionally by Chinese intellectuals: a sense of historical mission, an obligation to society, a concern for the fate of their nation. This is illustrated by a conspicuous slogan carried by the students occupying Tiananmen Square identifying themselves as *minzuhun* (the "soul of the nation"). This broad underlying commonality among the intellectuals of China still proves to be full of vitality in spite of so many frustrations.

Lin Tongqi also noted that there has been an influx of vast quantities of literature about the West regarding aesthetics, ethics, history, sociology, art, and philosophy. A new series of books that introduces Chinese readers to these Western concepts, *Toward the Future*, has sold ten million copies in the past four years. As a result, the Chinese are becoming more sophisticated about their ideas of the West and do not all have simplistic notions of the West. They are not satisfied with a global picture of Western culture as a single entity.

Peter Bol said that within Confucianism there should be a distinction between fields of activity and places to which people turn for values. He recalled a passage in the *Analects* where Confucius's disciples are divided into four fields, *sike (ssu-k'e):* government, speaking and conversation, cultural learning, and ethical conduct. Those continue to be used through the centuries, and at least three of them—cultural learning, government, and ethical conduct—were used to divide the areas of Confucian life. There are also questions of the sources for values. Heaven and earth is one, and antiquity and its texts is another. But all this leaves aside the question of religion. It is not simply that Protestantism is doing well in Asia; religious organizations generally are doing well. In Taiwan, for example, it seems likely that religious cults and ritual associations are growing faster than Protestant or Catholic churches. In mainland China, there is an enormous resurgence of Buddhist and Taoist organizations. This phenomenon seems very much outside the field of Confucianism; in the past, too, there were also movements toward cults, toward religious organizations outside Confucian concerns.

Carter Eckert noted that in Korea, with some 25–30 percent of the population calling itself Christian, the church has become deeply rooted and indigenous and has absorbed much of the Confucian tradition. Accordingly, it makes less sense to view it as outside the Confucian culture. Also, the question of whether there is a connection between the rise of Protestantism in Asia and economic growth cannot be answered without an examination of the entrepreneurial elements of society to see how deeply involved with the church they are. Eckert's sense is that in Korea this is not the case.

Wang Gungwu added that in the case of the Chinese in the Philippines, they became Catholics from the end of the sixteenth century; they always had to become Catholic if they wished be successful in business in the Spanish Philippines. However, over the centuries, this did not make them less Chinese, and while it did not impede business success, it seems less that they became good businessmen because they were Catholic and more that they became Catholics because they were good businessmen!

George De Vos said that he feels uneasy in discussing religious conversion without research into the reasons. For example, in a different context, Sicilians and Belgians are converting to Jehovah's Witnesses in large numbers. At first this seems strange, but upon a closer look it turns out that Catholicism in Belgium does not support the patriarchal position of the father in the family, whereas Jehovah's Witnesses do. There is change going on; people are discontented and looking for alternatives, but there may be a number of different movements going on at the same time with different segments of the population.

Terry Lautz asked, in view of events in Tiananmen Square, to what extent Confucianism has the capacity for democratic development and political reform.

Cultural Identity and Social Implications

GILBERT ROZMAN OPENED the third session by describing a research project he has been engaged in during the past three years with a number of faculty and graduate students at Princeton University together with some outsiders. The objective of the project has been to identify a systematic way of approaching the topic of cultural identity. The project, which will result in a book, has ended up emphasizing three themes. First, in an introductory section, the issue of what international perspective one might take on the East Asian region, viewed as one of three regions of rapid modernization in the world—the West, the "North" (the Russian tradition and the socialist path to modernization which grew out of it), and East Asia. Rozman's group sought to specify historical characteristics of each of the three types of modernization and their combinations.

The second, and core, section of the volume deals with the Confucianization of each of the three major East Asian areas. Patricia Ebrey wrote on Confucianization of China, emphasizing the further spread of Confucian ideas into social behavior in the late imperial era, especially from the Song to the Ming dynasties. JaHyun Kim Haboush wrote an account of the Confucianization of Korea, and Martin Colcott did a paper on the Confucianization of Japan and its limits, emphasizing the transition to the Tokugawa era. An attempt was made, albeit imprecisely, to measure the degree to which the societies in question had become Confucianized.

In the process the group became very aware of the extent to which the term *Confucianism* encompasses many different meanings. Accordingly, in the final part of the book, especially, an attempt was made to distinguish types of Confucianism. This section deals with the transition from the nineteenth century into the modern era, with one chapter comparing China and Japan and another (written by Michael Robinson) focusing on Korea. Since this classification seems to fit in well with the earlier discussion of types of discourse, Rozman considered it especially appropriate for the workshop's attention. He noted that he was viewing Confucianism more as a set of behavioral patterns than as a set of ideas.

The typology his group constructed was derived from the experiences of China and Japan in the last century. It includes the following levels:

1. *Imperial Confucianism,* which centered on ideology and ritual supportive of the emperor's rights and the delegated authority of those who exercised power on his behalf. Those who emphasize this aspect to the exclusion of others tend to see Confucianism as inherently conservative and supportive of government authority.

2. *Reform Confucianism,* which provided something of a counterbalance to this conservatism. For example, in Japan on three occasions in the eighteenth and first half of the nineteenth century there was an effort to reform society drawing on Confucian inspiration, with a special emphasis on corruption—the very theme the students in Beijing are focusing on at present, and in the tradition of the May Fourth Movement.

3. *Confucianism of social elites not holding high government posts,* which included among it members, in China, members of the scholar-official class and in Japan, the samurai. The latter should not be viewed merely as servants of the state, for they also had independence of thought.

4. *Merchant house Confucianism* (derived in part from Thomas Rohlen), which is a set of ideas about business organization. As Sam Yamashita has already indicated, this was one of the major methods by which Confucian elements of discourse spread in the Meiji period, especially in the early twentieth century.

5. *Mass Confucianism,* which was practiced by the general population, including vast numbers of peasants.

Rozman took as his task the comparison of China and Japan based on the strength of these categories. To summarize briefly: Imperial Confucianism was more dominant in China, but was less emphasized in Japan during the Tokugawa period. However, it remained in the background and was invoked in the 1860s and again in the 1880s and 1890s. In China it was so closely associated with the existing order and so much identified with Confucianism as a whole that its repudiation left relatively little room for other elements of Confucianism. On the other hand, Rozman views reform Confucianism as having been much weaker in Qing China than in Tokugawa Japan. It had already been invoked as a force there and could be reinvoked as the modern era began.

Elite Confucianism in Japan was transformed to involve *bushido* (the Way of the samurai); it combined a number of elements of a separate tradition, associated in part with Zen practices. Rozman emphasized his belief that understanding the differences in elite Confucianism between the two countries is important to understanding their different paths of development.

Merchant house Confucianism involved such values as gratitude, propriety, humility, understanding of hierarchy, and the practice of ancestor veneration. In Japan the separate *chonin bunka* (townspeople culture) helped provide a more solid foundation to elements of merchant house Confucianism. This can be seen in the Tokugawa era as well as the twentieth century (perhaps less so in the early Meiji era).

Mass Confucianism had spread earlier in China; Japan was catching up through education in Tokugawa, but still lagged behind.

Rozman concluded by suggesting ways to carry forward a systematic effort to study Confucianism through sociological themes. One would be to focus on periodization and stages of modernization and premodern development and to relate the nature of the society as it changes to the appeal of the various elements of Confucian thought.

A second task would be to distinguish further the types of Confucianism; a third would be to emphasize social classes and social institutions and examine how they interacted with the Confucian tradition. Of course, Confucianism is used here quite broadly. Certainly in both China and Japan there were many other elements to society; then, too, how people actually *perceived* institutions and ideals is an interesting issue. But Rozman would rather emphasize the question of what the *origins* of these were. In all three of the East Asian countries there is much in common in terms of the classics, the origins, the means by which Confucian thought was spread. Then, the next stage is to analyze what the social class system was that carried forth these ideas. That is, how did ideas interact with different social structures in the various countries of East Asia?

Thomas Gold started by suggesting that cultural identity implies a set of values and orientations held by individuals, collectivities and institutions. Also, cultural identity, as Rozman has indicated, was not uniform over time or place. From the outside, we see commonalities in East Asia; but when we scratch beneath the surface, we become aware of the great diversity of cultural identity given the rubric of Confucianism. This diversity within East Asia exists not just between the political units, but within them, as well, particularly *within* China. As discussed in the previous session, one of the main themes of *He shang* is the "yellow" areas of China versus the "blue" ones, that is, the river areas versus coastal-oriented regions. Also, it is important to distinguish between northern and southern China. Such diversity is caused by a variety of factors, but Gold recommends focusing on key variables such as topography, natural resources, and political events to understand how such differences in cultural identity are formed.

In Gold's understanding of the concept, cultural identity is a configuration of a number of different possible elements. Culture may be thought of as a tool kit that does not just define ultimate ends, but also defines "tools" (mentalities) by which people deal with the world and try to understand it.

Gold next raised a series of issues concerning the use of the concept of cultural identity. How can one measure cultural identity? And at what level? Is there a threshold at which one can determine, for example, that someone is a Confucian? That some society is Confucian in its identity? How many attributes of Confucianism are necessary before we can apply the term? Is it tied to a particular geographical area or to a type of socio-political system? In the case of overseas Chinese in Southeast Asia, Gold feels that they believed they were behaving in a very traditional manner, but they were operating in a very different socio-political system. Is their cultural identity still Confucian even though their success has been in the fourth of the four traditional occupational categories?

In capitalist East Asia, what seems to be happening is a shift from the emphasis of the elements of a "modal personality" within the Confucianism cultural identity. There are economic, social, and political aspects of this shift in the emphasis of different aspects of the tool kit of cultural identity. Different tools (i.e., aspects of the configuration) are emphasized based on situational factors. In places such as Taiwan, Korea, and Hong Kong we see the legitimation, or strengthening, of particular elements that were previously denigrated, as well as the introduction and successful incorporation of elements from outside. This then leads to the difficult question of how much we should attribute the success of capitalism in these countries to the influence of the Confucianism that was already present and how much we attribute to the various situational factors that have led to a particular development of Confucian elements.

When sociologists speak of personality, one concept they use is "role set." Individuals need to play many different roles in society; some of these are "master roles" while others are "minor roles." In Confucian culture there is an acceptance of the legitimacy of powerful individuals and groups determining the role set of individuals. That is, in the Confucian tradition the master role that people will play in their lives is determined less by the individual and more by other powerful individuals or groups. Confucian culture is hierarchical, and part of the process of socialization is learning to submerge oneself at many different levels. This submersion is a continuum from the micro level to the macro level, since an individual is a member of many different collectivities. Individuals in the various Confucian cultural areas use internal controls and direct external constraints to enforce submission.

This leads to another issue raised by *He shang* about the Confucian tradition, namely, its elective affinity for authoritarianism: the symbol of the dragon representing a symbol of submission to authority. Chinese intellectuals critical of Chinese tradition agree with Lucian Pye's analysis of the Chinese political tradition emphasizing the need for a strong authority figure and the affinity for authoritarianism.

Gold then discussed the major issue of the nature and shape that democratization and liberalization will take in Confucian societies. He noted that a recent trend has been for leaders in East Asia to manipulate the perceived affinity between Confucian tradition and authoritarianism. This is seen, for example, in the debate in China over "New Authoritarianism" where certain elements in the leadership have seized upon an interpretation of the economic success in Taiwan, Korea, and Singapore that emphasizes their authoritarian political nature. They argue that China does not need, and cannot tolerate, Western-style pluralist democracy, but requires instead a new form of authoritarianism. But Gold argues that authoritarianism, hierarchical submission, and group orientation are not very conducive to the privacy and spontaneity necessary for rapid economic development. Successful, sustained economic development requires a private sphere for accumulation, having title to resources, and allocation of resources based on private decisions. There must be the freedom to form alliances and connections among individuals and groups to pursue goals that they themselves have selected, to make decisions based on a wide range of data, and to enjoy the rewards and bear the responsibilities based on their own personal decisions.

What seems to be happening in capitalist East Asia is that the cultural identity now includes the legitimacy of entrepreneurship, based not just on the individual as expected in the West, but also on the family. Because of various situational factors, entrepreneurship and privacy have been strengthened within capitalist East Asia. What we see happening in Taiwan, Korea, and somewhat in Singapore and Hong Kong is the emergence of civil society in the sense of free, spontaneous, and self-determined relationships among individuals and groups outside of the state. These sorts of relationships, derived from the development of private economy, are creating a fundamental change in the social and political structures of those societies. These changes have not come from top-down, conscious transformative policies, but are part of a long process of change with its own logic.

Referring to an earlier question by Terry Lautz concerning the relation between economic and political development, Gold noted that in the case of capitalist East Asia he believes there is a very clear relationship between these various forms of interpersonal relations that have derived from capitalist economic activity and political demands that have been arising.

Chang Hao spoke on the nature of cultural identity in modern China. Chang noted that when Joseph Levenson first raised the issue he discussed it mainly in terms of an emotional complex that Chinese intellectuals developed in their humiliating competition with the West. Chang would prefer to shift the focus and discuss the issue in the context of the intellectual changes that occurred in modern China. He argued that cultural identity did not become an issue with the Chinese until central cultural values were dislocated. Such conceptual dislocation occurred largely in the transitional period from 1895 to 1920 due the following developments. First, during that period, the core values of imperial Confucianism, embodying the doctrine of the three bonds *(sangang)*, came under vehement attack beginning in 1895 and reaching a peak during the May Fourth Movement in 1919. Second, other parts of the Confucian value system, such as the "Confucian ethics of virtue" (MacIntyre's term), also suffered serious erosion. The third development is that this disintegration of the Confucian value pattern was accompanied by a crackup of the Confucian worldview, which in various forms grew out of the Confucian doctrine of the meeting of heaven and man. Thus the conceptual dislocation that occurred in this era involved a dissolution of not only the basic value patterns, but also central worldviews. In Chang's view, it was a change of this magnitude that gave rise to two serious cultural crises: the crisis of cultural identity and the crisis of meaning. These two crises, along with the conceptual dislocation that gave rise to them, constitute an "orientational" crisis which began during that period and has continued down to the present. Thus, Chang argues, the issue of cultural identity needs to be seen as part of this broader crisis of orientation, which has marked the Chinese in the twentieth century.

Chang concluded by posing a question to the conference: Has this crisis of cultural identity gone further than those of other non-Western cultures in their own confrontations with the West? He noted that toward the end of the transitional period, the May Fourth Movement had been launched with an avowed purpose of rejecting the Chinese tradition as a whole. This sort of radical iconoclasm has come to dominate the Chinese intellectual cultural outlook from May Fourth down to the present. The popularity of *He shang* in the PRC and the writers Li Ao and Bo Yang in Taiwan are testimony to this outlook. This sort of mainstream radical rejection of the past is hard to find in the confrontation of other cultural groups (such as Hindu and Japanese) with the West. This radical cultural self-critique seems almost a unique phenomenon in the modern world.

DISCUSSION

Wang Gungwu noted that the agonizing and suffering over Confucianism really comes from the *shidafu* (*shih-ta-fu,* literati) class. The other classes do not appear to have the same worries. In effect, we are speaking of a tiny minority of the Chinese people who are continually worried and unhappy about their position vis-à-vis the great tradition. If we consider the merchants, we find there is a historical dimension. It seems fair to say that when the merchants came out from under the direct influence of *shidafu* members, they felt that they were as Chinese and Confucian as they had been in China. Although they may not have always appreciated all the fine points, they felt they had imbibed and absorbed enough of the tradition to be respectable. Outside of China over many generations, their perception of what Confucianism was would diminish; what they would retain would be very simple ritualism, symbolic fragments of the tradition which they did not fully understand. When one looks at the generations of the *pranakan* in Indonesia or the *baba* in Malaysia, there have been many generations of Chinese from the seventeenth or eighteenth century onward. Or those who have been intermarrying with Filipinas in the Philippines or Thais in Thailand—most of them would have very little understanding of what Confucianism meant. But they would retain certain aspects of Chinese customs, popular religious symbols, and so forth, to demonstrate that they were still Chinese: they would keep their Chinese surname, practice certain burial rituals and observe certain festivals, and wear Chinese clothes on certain occasions. They would not read or speak Chinese, but nevertheless they identified themselves as some kind of Chinese. The question of being Chinese and being Confucian was not a great problem for them: as long as they thought they were Chinese, they never doubted being Confucian. Their standards of being Chinese were quite relaxed.

The trouble only began when the literati returned; this started only in the late nineteenth century when Qing China began to recognize these overseas Chinese, claiming them and giving them nationality, a concept that had never been there before. Especially after 1909 when a nationality law was enacted, officials were sent from China to make sure that their "Chineseness" was satisfactory. Essentially, a decision was made to re-Sinify these overseas Chinese by setting up schools, teaching them Chinese, making sure that they would rise steadily toward the heights expected of any genuine Chinese. This outside imposition of culture began in the late Qing and continued right through the Guomindang period up to the 1950s until nationalism in southeast Asia created a new situation. It was easy to do this since the colonial governments were not legitimate in the eyes of the Chinese—they had no right to tell the Chinese how to behave. What was surprising was these overseas Chinese were divided between those who very readily accepted these new higher standards of Chineseness and those who did not. From the point of view of the literati, these were "lost" and no longer Chinese; hence they were no problem. But those who still clung to their Chinese identity found themselves in a vulnerable position, branded as inferior Chinese with the imperative to do something about it. They had preserved portions of Chinese culture in the local languages. For example, there was a great amount of Chinese literature written in Malay, including *Sanguo yani* (Romance of the Three Kingdoms), local drama. This had helped them identify with China, and the fact that it was not in the Chinese language never bothered them. But with the reimposition of higher standards of being Chinese, including obtaining a Chinese passport, problems of the degree to which they were Chinese were raised. And it is remarkable how responsive, on the whole, they were.

When it was put to them that being Chinese did not require being Confucian, they were very upset. The post-May Fourth Guomindang education officials did not much emphasize Confucianism, and many of the older generation of Chinese in Southeast Asia resented this. In Indonesia, Confucianism was actually established as a *religion,* especially after Kang Youwei's (K'ang Yu-wei) visit to Java, which is still alive today. It is one of the official religions recognized by the Indonesian government and is the way by which they maintained an identity as Chinese. In the 1910s all the "Four Books" were translated into Indonesian and now are read. In Suravaya, which is the headquarters of the Confucian church, they have made films for circulation among the Chinese communities in Indonesia on what it means to be a religious Confucian. What is remarkable is that all the rituals of this church are conducted very much in Christian forms: there are sermons, they meet weekly, they have a proper church organization, and so forth. It should be noted, however, that the membership of this church is a small minority of the Chinese in Indonesia; it is not particularly popular. Indeed, there are more Chinese who are Catholics and Protestants than adherents to the Confucian church.

This is an illustration of the complexity of being Chinese. These people have never been to China, they do not speak Chinese or have anything to do with anyone who does speak Chinese, but among themselves they have continued a tradition of Chineseness. This is rather akin, perhaps, to the case of the Jews in Kaifeng. Recently, Wang noted, he had been a member of a group of fifteen scholars who had held a conference on Chinese identities and published a volume from the proceedings. In the course of their investigations, they were surprised by the large number of identities involved. Of these, nationality is only one, but is perhaps the most interesting. It has a very recent history, for it was not until the middle of the nineteenth century that any Chinese thought of nationality at all. This began because in the treaty ports the British consuls decided that they should protect British-born Chinese, for example, those born in strait settlements of Penang, Singapore, and Malacca, as British subjects. Back in Xiamen (Amoy), Ningbo, and elsewhere, their brushes with the law fell under extraterritoriality. This created a big problem with the Chinese government. From this time on, the subject came up constantly in all relations between the Chinese government and foreign powers and finally led to the Nationality Act of 1909. Strictly speaking, this law arose from a debate with the Dutch East Indies over this issue. The Dutch maintained that every person born in the Dutch East Indies was a Dutch subject and that therefore the Chinese government had no rights over any overseas Chinese residing there. The Chinese government refused to accept this, thus bringing about an argument that lasted some ten years. The conclusion was that they would be Dutch subjects when in the Dutch East Indies and Chinese subjects when in China. The Nationality Act of 1909 dictated that as long as one was born of a Chinese father, then upon arriving in China he or she would be Chinese. Outside of China, the issue of nationality would be negotiable. This led to an emotional issue among the Chinese of this generation, and many chose to defy Dutch law and insist that they were Chinese even in the Dutch East Indies.

When independence came to the former colonies in Southeast Asia the issue again arose. That generation of Chinese thought it extremely shameful and humiliating to give up their Chinese nationality and take up the new nationalities. By the 1970s and 1980s the issue had become unimportant. Chinese are going everywhere and taking up foreign nationalities (e.g., Hong Kong residents fleeing abroad). For them, there is a new sense that nationality has nothing to do with their identity. This marks a major transition in the evolution of Chinese identity, all the more remarkable that it has occurred in the space of a single generation.

In conclusion, Wang stated that a key consideration is whether the Chinese feel that there is a center or not. There was a time in the Ming and early Qing period when, for these overseas Chinese, there was no center, since the Chinese governments did not recognize them as Chinese. When there was no center, they had no problem with their identity; they privately considered themselves Chinese. When a center came about through the efforts of the late Qing and Guomindang governments, then the problem became serious and they all responded. The fact that they are not doing so today suggests a perception that there is no center of Chineseness and therefore being Chinese can be anything. It is a private matter, an issue of personal identity. There is no China which is the center, to which one must respond.

George De Vos asked whether it is possible for a foreigner to become Chinese.

Wang responded that it is relatively easy in the PRC, if you are of Chinese extraction, to become a Chinese citizen, though dual nationality has been not recognized since the New Nationality Law was enacted in 1981. For someone not of Chinese extraction, the process is more complicated. Taiwan, on the other hand, has not done away with the 1909 law, so that all people who have a Chinese father are considered eligible for ROC citizenship, whatever their passport.

De Vos asked if this was not something of a racial definition.

Wang said that the operative term is *minzu (min-tzu)*.

Tu Weiming noted that he did not believe that being Chinese was necessarily ethnic, for there are some fifty million members of minority groups in China, including Tibetans.

De Vos asked whether or not it was conceptually difficult to imagine that a Caucasian could become Chinese.

Wang stated that in his view it would be very difficult.

Richard Madsen pointed out that among those who had sympathized with the revolution were Caucasians such as George Hatem and Sidney Shapiro. They have been esteemed by the Chinese state and given state funerals.

Peter Bol offered a general comment. He noted that Wang Gungwu had illustrated how cultural identity is really a historical phenomenon and that, in fact, part of the whole notion of Confucianism as part of the Chinese identity is a historical creation. While listening to the presentations by the two sociologists, Bol said that he had been struck by the feeling that they were using the word *Confucianism* in ways very close to meaning "the traditional Chinese socio-political order and the values thereof." Bol holds, that to some degree, it is precisely because there is a sense of discontinuity with the Chinese past that we in the West have created the notion of Confucianism as a way to address the issue of cultural connections between pre-Western and post-Western China: something central in the Chinese cultural identity. In listening to Rozman and Gold, Bol found himself to be confused as to their meaning of Confucianism. Thus in Rozman's five categories, could not the word *culture* be substituted for Confucianism? If we say that it does not really matter whether people perceive it as Confucian or not and that it is really a historical question of its origins, then we could point out that the classics antedate Confucius and ask what is Confucian with them. Bol then questioned whether we want to make a distinction between Chinese culture and Confucianism, or between the traditional Chinese socio-political order and Confucianism, and if so, how do we make it? Also, he asked Rozman and Gold exactly what they mean when they speak of "Confucian values."

Rozman responded that there are three ways of attempting to identify whether a pattern is Confucian or not. (1) *The intellectual origins:* Can it be traced to the classics or to the ideals of Confucian thinkers? (2) *How people perceive them:* Do people identify them as part of the Confucian tradition in some way? (3) *Latent social patterns:* Are there social patterns of an institution which, even though they may not be perceived as such, can be traced back to earlier Confucian ideas or ways of organizing? Rozman's belief is that for both Japan and China, all those types of Confucian that he detailed can meet at least the third of these criteria, if not the first or second.

Tu related the story of how Yamasaki Anzai, in seventeenth-century Japan, asked his students the hypothetical question of how they would respond if Confucius, as the commanding general, with seventy-two disciples as lieutenants and his three thousand students, began to invade Japan. Some students said that Confucius is against aggressive warfare, so this would not be possible. When Yamasaki insisted they consider the hypothetical possibility, other students felt that Confucius would only engage in righteous warfare, so therefore we would be wrong. But Yamasaki said that his answer was that it was against the Confucian principle to invade a foreign country. Accordingly, Yamasaki Anzai was identifying himself as a Confucian, but not with Chinese culture. Thus, Confucianism as a form of thought, as a way of life, as a spiritual orientation, on the one hand is narrower than Chinese culture, which is a much broader term; but at the same time, it is broader than Chinese culture. Another example is from Yi T'oegye when he noted how the contemporary Confucians in Ming China were failing to understand the great project of Zhu Xi, and that it was his responsibility as true Confucian to continue the Zhu Xi line.

Another issue is that of things Confucian which happened before Confucius. This is easier to understand if we take into consideration Judaism rather than just Christianity and Buddhism. While it is impossible to be more Christian than Jesus Christ or be more Buddhist than Sakyamuni, a Jew can compare himself as a Jew to Moses and can discuss Jewish ideas and traditions prior to Moses. Confucius certainly was a very important transmitter, but in the Confucian tradition itself he does not represent the highest manifestation of Confucian ideal. Yao and Shun, as the sage kings, could be considered more Confucian than Confucius.

Schwartz noted that some of his earlier remarks were relevant to this discussion, especially his notion that Confucianism means having certain texts and pondering about these common cultural orientations. When one identifies Confucianism with Chinese culture as a whole, one also identifies Chinese culture with Confucianism. But there have been marked anti-Confucian trends in Chinese thought. Zhuang Zi (Chuang Tzu), for example, radically rejects the notion of the salvational role of the political order. Also, one might cite the differences between Legalists such as Han Fei Zi and those such as the "eight schools of *ru*" whom he attacks, and the Moists, who in many ways depart from what might be called basic Chinese cultural traits. So Schwartz defended his use of the term *Confucian* on the grounds that he wants to have the possibility of recognizing that there are in China people who run against the general cultural tendency. The fact that it is vague and that its outlines are not so clear is not unlike the case of Hinduism in India. Even in the case of Western Christianity, we are dealing with a tremendously complicated tradition, ranging from Greek Orthodoxy to New England Unitarianism. Is all this part of one religion? They do still appeal to one set of common scriptures. To be sure, adherents of deconstructionism might ask what scriptures have in common: with ten interpreters you get ten interpretations. For all these reasons, in a broad, vague way Schwartz would prefer to identify something called Confucianism.

Madsen underscored the reality of Confucianism by noting that the vehemence with which Confucianism is rejected in China suggests that people are still captive to it. If, rather than rejecting it angrily, they rejected it by not caring at all then it has no importance. Those in China involved in tearing down Confucianism seem caught in a Confucian *problematique*.

De Vos maintained that when we speak of Chinese culture we mean a clan system with a patrilineal organization. When we look at Japan and Korea and ask when they became Confucianist, then perhaps we are getting at what Confucianism is. In De Vos's view, it is a certain form of social hierarchy that comes out of the hierarchy of the family, the establishment of social relationships within the family, and a definition of family. The secondary definition, the political definition of a polity or some sort of political structuring may come and go in different ways; people can remain culturally Confucian without the overarching political structure. But if their family structure changes, then they are no longer Confucian. Somewhere in the definition of family relationships and a sense of hierarchy that comes out of these relationships is a general area to examine when providing a definition of what is Confucian and what is not Confucian. Second, there is a concept of life trajectory (more on this during De Vos's presentation later), which concerns the person through time. This, De Vos held, is an essential part of what it means to be Confucian.

Bol asked how it is known that this is an essential part of being Confucian?

De Vos replied that it is also linked with the family structure, especially the hierarchy based on age, that is, an age-grading system, which is, in De Vos's view, an essential part of Confucian thought.

Bol said that if we know from the results of investigations of the Shang dynasty that the clan system already existed in ancient China, then what De Vos is really speaking of is an "ur-pattern" of Chinese culture. It certainly is true that the *ru* and other scholars of antiquity thought that the family was important, even while being critical in many ways of certain practices. But this, he maintained, does not make the family Confucian. And just because they thought hierarchy legitimate does not make hierarchy Confucian. It makes hierarchy something that Confucians feel is legitimate.

De Vos believes that all of these elements can be seen separately in other contexts. It is the combination of these elements in some variety of molecular organization that becomes specifically Confucian. You can take all these elements and find them in other systems; but their combination produces a culture pattern related organizationally to society that stems from the family and treats aging in a certain way. This, De Vos maintains, is the core of the Confucian ethos. It is the ordering of people, one with another, in a particular fashion that defines Confucianism.

James Watson noted that scholars who study the Chinese family tend to be very cynical about that organization having any kind of Confucian roots at all. The more they take apart the Chinese family, the more critical they tend to be of the whole notion of Confucianism. This view will be presented in more detail later in the conference, but obviously there is something critical about the Chinese, the Korean family, indeed, the East Asian family. But Watson posed the question, what about the Punjabi family? The Punjabi Sikh family has many of the same structures and features as those Watson himself studied, but few would argue that the Punjabi Sikhs have a Confucian family system! De Vos's notion of the molecular construction of the Chinese family seems appropriate. When you examine each of the constituent atoms, scholars become cynical; yet somehow we are left with something. The whole of Confucianism is a mirage.

Tu was reminded of his visit to the University of Punjab, where he gave a lecture. Some of the leading Sikh scholars were very pleased and remarked, "Ah, this is exactly what we're thinking about!" They subsequently had a long conversation concerning shared value orientations. And then they showed him all the pictures of the Sikh sages, all of them with swords on horseback. It was then, Tu noted, that he realized that even though there may be points of convergence, further exploration will show a much more complex picture.

Gender and Family

GEORGE DE VOS BEGAN by observing that how women fit into Confucian society is a topic often neglected. This raises questions about early education and about differences between patriarchal societies in East Asia and those in, for example, the Mediterranean, where there is a different sort of family system. Though both are patriarchal, there are important differences. To help explain this, the issue of the internalization of culture by women needs to be addressed.

Also, when there is generational revolt, how do we understand what is happening? During the revolt at Berkeley in the 1960s, there was a philosopher named Feuer who wrote a book on generational revolts (Lewis S. Feuer, *The Conflict of Generations: The Character and Significance of Student Movements*). In the end, he left Berkeley, for he did not like what was happening. De Vos found the book to be too heavily laden with the structure of standard psychoanalysis; his central explanation for the appearance of revolt involved only sons rebelling against fathers. This, he felt, left out the major question of where women are in generational revolt. Also, what is being conveyed to children by women? In *Bungei shunju,* for example, there was an article that described how women were seen passing out candy to revolting students. What is the relationship of women's attitudes toward revolt when it appears? Or, toward continuity? How does the woman's role, or the internalization of the woman's role, relate to cultural continuity of family experiences? At least from the Japanese standpoint, women really got internalized somewhere in the public educational system following the Meiji reforms.

Looking at anthropological approaches, one finds in Edward Norbeck's work with older people in Japanese villages in the 1950s (e.g., *Takashima, a Japanese Fishing Village,* 1954) that many of the changes in customs came in after public education. Before that time, people were not Confucian; the ethical education in the schools based on the Imperial Rescript on Education was responsible for this change. There was a universalization of education that penetrated into the rural communities that had their own customs.

De Vos next posed a related question: how do Confucian attitudes get transmitted within the matrix of the family? He cited comparative research on the school systems of the United States, Japan, and Taiwan which indicates that, despite arrogant assumptions that we are teaching how to think in u.s. schools, on any objective scale the Japanese are doing better in science and math and that even the best school in Minnesota ranks below a Japanese mediocre one. In yet another study, in this case a report of psychological tests of "field dependence" and "field independence" related to cognitive development, the Japanese also do much better than do Americans. In general, in tests of this kind, where they can be compared, the Japanese come out very much better than do Americans. What is going on here in socialization?

Such socialization begins quite early, and the mother is the day-to-day early mentor for the child, passing on certain attitudes. De Vos, in this context, touched upon the issue of rote learning, noting that we in the West have come to assume in recent pedagogy that there is nothing to be gained by rote learning. Perhaps this is an underestimation of the value of rote learning, viewed as a part of an educational progression. Rote learning begins quite early in Japan, and De Vos approvingly commented that bowing training is as important as bowel training in early education, that the comportment of the body is something that, if exercised properly, gives pleasure, but also makes one feel moral. What, then, is there in the practice of ritual that gives one a sense of righteousness, of goodness? In the United States we tend to overlook this, because we cannot understand it ourselves. Indeed, De Vos feels that scholars in particular do not like ritual and do not appreciate it.

As an example of ritual learning, consider the tea ceremony in Japan. It has no content; it teaches no moral statement. And yet it has a certain quality of sacredness about it. For those who are adept, it gives genuine pleasure. The concepts of aesthetics and righteousness, in De Vos's opinion, have certain kinds of motoric base which are acquired in early learning. In the ideal Confucianism, at least, self-control starts very early and is developed throughout the life trajectory.

What is life about in Japan? There are, De Vos noted, some instrumentalizations of goals that go on. From the age of six or seven, progressive demands are made on children. Also important is the issue of who is doing what in front of the children. There is an example being dramatized in the Confucian family. If it is working, ideally there is a presentation of self-sacrifice toward eventual goals in the person of the mother and in the mother's interpretation of what the father is doing, if she is playing her role well in this system. There is a hierarchical system built around age grading. Implicit in the system is the notion that empowerment or the actualization of the self is long-range and eventual, rather than immediate.

In De Vos's understanding of the term, these qualities of being are very much part of the Confucian system. The Confucian experience in Japan is no longer taught as Confucianism, but it is still experienced. Early socialization within a type of family in which there is role behavior of a certain kind, which is hierarchical, but one which indicates there is an advantage to waiting and enduring for future gratification—all this is counter, in De Vos's mind, to the current situation in America, where desire for instant gratification is the rule. Those families that come out of the Confucian tradition, including those we loosely term the "middle class," have women who, to some degree, have internalized a certain form of role behavior that gives them a type of approach to children that socializes them very well in the modern world.

De Vos ended on an empirical note by relating how since the early 1950s, he has been using the Thematic Apperception Tests (TAT). In the high schools of Japan, the card showing a boy looking at a violin lying on a table, the boy is still playing the violin and not escaping to go outdoors and play baseball as are most American boys. The violin playing is internalized and the main concern is whether the boy can play. In the Japanese boys' answers, the boy still works hard and in the end he becomes adept in playing the violin. In the American case, the mother is seen as making the boy play the violin; he wants to play baseball. It used to be that in the middle class the boy would reluctantly play the violin, while in the lower class the boy would go out and play baseball as soon as the mother was gone. Now, more and more middle-class boys are answering that the boy will go out and play baseball. There is a sad note coming into the middle-class answers: the boy is looking at the violin and maybe would like to learn to play it, but there is no one there to teach him.

Roderick MacFarquhar related a comment of Daniel Okimoto (author of *MITI and the Market: Japanese Industrial Policy for High Technology*). When asked how, if ever, the Japanese success story might break down, he responded that it would happen if the women ever stopped staying at home and educating the children and stopped getting them through the exams. MacFarquhar feels that the gender question needs to be examined in greater depth in all the East Asian countries.

James Watson commented on the violin TAT picture. Nearly twenty years ago he used them in field work in the New Territories of Hong Kong. The violin picture elicited the response from ordinary villagers, "How much?"

Ezra Vogel, following up on MacFarquhar's remark, gave the Singapore response to the question of how the society might fail. In a conversation in the summer of 1988, Prime Minister Lee Kwan Yew expressed regret that they had not followed the Japanese example and kept the well-educated women at home. In the long run, the most important problems are eugenics and providing good training for the children in order to build a strong society.

Henry Rosovsky asked Vogel to elaborate on how the exam system works for selecting politicians.

Vogel described how the PAP party in Singapore (which almost always wins) selects politicians for its constituencies. The criteria used are overwhelmingly meritocratic, perhaps because the leaders of Singapore themselves had risen through examinations. Almost without exception, the candidates selected compose a roster of the students who did the best in their class at university.

Benjamin Schwartz commented that ritual in Confucianism is very much tied into ritualism as it relates to roles, and therefore hierarchy and status. But in the West we are all the inheritors of the Enlightenment ideal of getting rid of all hierarchy and status in human society. Schwartz confessed that he shared the Western prejudices against hierarchy and authority. But it is important to understand a different mindset where people take pride in living within the hierarchical station in which they find themselves. Even in the West, this was the case in, say, Shakespeare's work: hierarchy, status, and authority are accepted. And the need for hierarchy, status, authority, and rote behavior in our society may be a fact that we cannot live up to. In this respect, perhaps, the nations of East Asia are more honest.

De Vos agreed, lamenting that in America no distinction is made between *authority* and *authoritarian,* presenting us with a dilemma. A second dilemma is whether or not Confucianism can be modernized. For even if we accept the need for certain forms of hierarchy and age gradations, what should we do about hierarchy within the family? Just as in the world of Islam, where an important issue is whether the scriptures can be reinterpreted to revise the position of women, can the Confucian scriptures provide for a different view of women's role in society?

Tu Weiming responded that of all the Confucian values that have received vehement criticism since the May Fourth Movement, the so-called three bonds can be singled out. These represent three types of domination: father over son (age), husband over wife (gender), ruler over minister (status authority). Because of the attack on the three bonds by the modern intellectuals in East Asia, there has also been dissatisfaction with the five relationships. Recently Tu has reexamined this issue and tried to make a clear distinction between the two. To Tu's surprise, the *locus classicus* for the three bonds is the Legalist text of *Han Fei Zi* (although it is also mentioned briefly in the *Xun Zi* (Hsün Tzu) and is quite marginal in the Confucian classical tradition. The five relationships, however, are more important and appear in *Mencius.* If we examine them, we find the parent/child relationship based on age and authority, the ruler/minister relationship based on status authority, the husband/wife relationship based not on authority, but on division of labor, the older brother/younger brother relationship based on age, and the friend/friend relationship based on trust. Many Confucian scholars, in responding to the criticisms of the three bonds, decided to reduce these relationships to one: friendship. Such reformulations were seen as early as the seventeenth century, but the most famous of such treatments was that of Kang Youwei in the late nineteenth century. If we take status, gender, authority, and hierarchical structure seriously, we really must examine the logic of the five relationships, even though the three bonds are totally outdated. One very important feature of this logic is to say that each of the relationships is based on a value that is not totally transferrable. Each of the five relationships has its own inner logic which is not transferable. For example, the father/son relationship is a natural bonding, which cannot be disowned. The ruler/minister relationship, however, is voluntary association: if the ruler is not righteous, one can criticize him, or leave, or even launch a revolution. In sum, Tu feels that the five relationships should not be thrown out with the three bonds, but should be examined further for the perspective of reciprocity.

Peter Bol turned to the question of ritual, maintaining that Ogyu Sorai's assertion that the Japanese truly had something of ancient China that the Chinese had lost was correct. Certainly, he noted, ritual as a conceptual device for looking at social organizations works much better with Japan than with China. The ultimate realization of the ideal of ritual may be seen as the Japanese company. However, within ritual there are different varieties of relationships. Among Chinese thinkers on ritual, for example, there are those who strongly emphasize *shangxia zhifen (shang-hsia chih fen)*, the distinction between upper and lower. There are others, just as committed to the idea of ritual, who do not wish to talk of this at all, but who instead envision a more organic order where there might be a center with "spokes" radiating outward connecting people, with much less emphasis on hierarchy and authority. Another aspect of ritual that comes up is the notion that everyone must have a place. Once the situation is created where everyone must have a place, then it is possible to leave aside the question of hierarchy to some extent, since what matters is that one is playing a role, and this can be emphasized even where hierarchies exist. So there are a number of options.

Bol then posed a question to De Vos. When speaking of the role of the mother in the family, did he think it possible for this role to be taken up by family tutors and so forth? One's impression of elite society in China was that mothers did not necessarily have all that much contact with their children; for example, they also had wet nurses. The responsibility for inculcating norms, for their education, and so forth does not seem to have been borne necessarily by blood kin, but by hired help.

De Vos responded by pointing to the analogy of nineteenth-century Britain, where on the elite level there was a similar situation, but European. This raises the question of how one can have continuity and role playing and so on within a system in which the actual mother is someone else. The British case brings up some indelicate issues of class not spoken of often. In Victorian London there were several hundred thousand prostitutes. This fact is related to the issue at hand, since it involves sexuality and the ease of expression of sexuality towards someone of your own class. In a hierarchical system there may be affectional relationships with someone who is close, such as a wet nurse, but status relationships with women in a different way. Marriage may not be a matter of sexual attraction but rather status consideration; sexuality can be transferred elsewhere. De Vos suspects that in the Chinese system there was something of this situation. This is exemplified, for example, in the film *The Last Emperor,* where Pu Yi is shown as attached to his wet nurse. Also De Vos brought up the issue of suicide in Japan, citing his research with Hiroshi Wagatsuma into the question of the suicide of famous Japanese authors. They discovered that in every single instance the author had not been raised by his own mother, something that is unusual in Japan. All this raises a series of issues: How does continuity occur in an elite system? What are the prices paid? How is it better when a child is raised by the mother and not someone else? Does this cause a certain circulation of the elite to occur, if we see children raised by their own mothers as more likely to succeed? De Vos suspects that there is indeed a price paid for being an elite.

MacFarquhar pointed out that in the British system, within the elite families where the mother does not function as a "Japanese mother," two things prevail: the nanny is herself trained in training schools, which implant within them a certain loyalty to elite values, and the preparatory school (primary school). The instilling of education comes from the school system taking on the role of urging the pupil forward. It is not clear in the Japanese system who will take on this role if the mother does not.

Rosovsky observed that whenever assertions were made in the discussion concerning Confucian-style societies, he thinks of Europe and the United States and sees the differences as gradations, and even very subtle gradations. Concerning Schwartz's earlier remarks, he said that he feels hierarchy should be treated as a dynamic entity that moves up and down, rather than something that is unidirectional. The United States, for example, in its early history, probably consciously worked against certain aspects of hierarchy. But today,

Rosovsky believes, we have become an extremely hierarchical society. He expressed his interest in the economic consequences of "knowing your place" and noted Ian Buruma's observation that one of the most beautiful sights in Japan is to see a girl in a department store wrap a package. She knows her place, and she really tries to do the job as well as possible. That, Rosovsky feels, is what is so often missing in Western societies, especially in our recent, more disorganized phase. He wonders if this is not one of the beneficial aspects of a more hierarchical structure. One can even see this in universities. The situation where, for example, the professoriate views itself as having certain general obligations that include doing what one likes to do and what one does not like to do is very different from the American system, where we may pursue areas where rewards are thought to lie, forgetting obligations.

Tu Weiming, returning to De Vos's remarks on continuity, noted that De Vos and Walter Slote are co-editing a collection of essays on the psycho-cultural dynamics of the Confucian family in China, Japan, and Korea. One issue raised in this context is dependency need or emotional attachment. This is changing rather rapidly at present. In the 1980s the relationship, the bonding, between parent and child in Japan, Taiwan, and Korea remains a very long time. That is, the problem of how to become an independent adult in these societies, especially among the elite, is a pressing one. Usually the ties are not really cut off even when entering college. According to one of the reports in the *New York Times* on the demonstrations in Beijing, one of the students, just before fainting, lamented that he should never have told his mother what he was doing; he was concerned about his mother's anxiety over his political act. Such an attitude is very common among the students in Taiwan and Korea as well. Tu was reminded of a conversation with Erik Erikson concerning the question of being an adult. The Chinese term for "adult" is *chengren (ch'eng-jen)*, literally "to become a person." It is an achieved state, but it is not static; it is also evolving. In this case, no matter how old you are, even in your forties and fifties, when you confront your parents, again the special role, the bonding, returns. Thus, some critics ridicule the twenty-four diagrams of filial piety. One of the stories concerns a man in his sixties or early seventies who is trying to entertain his parents in their nineties by acting like a child. Most would now consider this story not only childish, but also distasteful. But within that cultural context it is very important and actually can generate some sympathetic response.

Schwartz noted how the discussion had touched upon the element of self-cultivation within Confucianism. This has within it an element of individuality, but one conceived of quite differently. While neither praising it nor blaming it, he pointed out that one becomes a fully developed individual within the Confucian tradition by playing all one's roles splendidly. When in a subordinate position, one plays that role splendidly, and similarly when in a superordinate position. This does not, in Schwartz's opinion, necessarily mean dependence, but rather is interdependence. However, there are some problems with this, even within Chinese thought. There is one school of thought that is very behavioristic: what makes you a splendid individual is just going through all these motions. There is also an opposing school, the Mencian school, which holds that you have to bring something to this behavior, something from inside. This is one of the great *problematiques* of Chinese thought, and it was quite resolved, that is, the relationship between the inner state of mind and external behavior.

De Vos pointed out that this issue is also a matter of debate in the theater. Laurence Olivier held that if you behave a certain way, then you come to be in the role, while others believe that you have to feel it, you must get into the mood and the person, and only then can you play the role. This debate is never-ending.

Bol said that everyone who has been in China and Japan is struck by the fact that Japanese people in department stores wrap packages well and that people in Chinese department stores do not wrap them. Or if they do, they wrap them badly. People in subordinate positions in China are unhappy about being in those positions; this is not just true on the mainland, but also true, to a large extent, in Taiwan as well. If we are assuming that ritual, hierarchy, and ideas of role are in some sense part of a Sinic tradition, a Confucian tradition, even, that lives on in contemporary Japan, then we might ask why it disappeared in China. I wonder if perhaps the sociologists could explain this?

By the way, Rosovsky asked, do we assume that once, say five hundred years ago, in China they wrapped the packages nicely?

Bol confessed that he was uncertain of this, of whether things changed in the seventeenth and eighteenth centuries, when the massive population increase came about and society in general deteriorated, leading to civil war, and so on, or maybe it never existed in China anyway.

Thomas Gold noted that perhaps it would be better to focus on the notion of craftsmanship, rather than package wrapping, which is a menial task. You can still find some sectors in the PRC where people take pride in their craft. But among people in positions that have low pay and low respect in China, you will find the typical package wrapper in a Chinese department store. So perhaps this is not quite the right kind of analogy since the Japanese package wrapper is accorded a certain amount of respect and does earn a livable wage.

Community and Education

RODERICK MACFARQUHAR OPENED the session by observing that the previous day the task had been an attempt to define what the "Confucian citizen" was, what his ethical world was, and how he attempted to update that world, whether to reject it in the modern world. Basically the concern was the individual Confucian in his or her own world. Today the workshop will focus on the Confucian more in relation to others, both in the community sphere and the political sphere. As recent events in East Asia have demonstrated, the adaptation to the modern world of political systems created by peoples strongly enthused by Confucian values has not proceeded as smoothly as they might have wanted. Clearly there are great differences between the conditions that have prevailed in Beijing, Tokyo, and Seoul in recent times, but all of them suggest that the adaptation of the political structure, which was in the homeland of Confucianism the great achievement for so many years, has not been as successful as would have been desired. MacFarquhar drew a distinction between the high Confucian culture of the elite, many of whom expected to go into government and identified many of their interests with those of the state, and the much more vulgarized, much more attenuated, much more simplified Confucianism of society-at-large, what was the previous day termed "bourgeois Confucianism." MacFarquhar felt that the reasons for holding this workshop lie, in part at least, in the success of certain aspects of the inheritors of the Confucian tradition in certain spheres—such as community, education, and family—and the impact that has had upon their ability to cope with the challenges of modernization.

Ezra Vogel said that reflecting on the question of social institutions growing out of Confucianism and thinking of which ones might appropriately belong in that category, one that stands out is the use of entrance examinations, and particularly the use of entrance examinations to select officials. In China, the examination for long existed down to the local level. The state did not attempt to set up a universal school system; rather the examinations were used for selecting elite officials. It had, as well, a number of subsidiary functions such as setting a standard of national culture that penetrated to the local level, thus providing in a very heterogeneous country a common culture. Those who did not pass often played a very prominent role in the local community and provided linkages with the officials. Accordingly, the examination system had a great deal of impact apart from its main purpose of selecting officials meritocratically. If one thinks about the modern examination system, the odd paradox is that the country that started the modern examination system (that is, focused on modern contents, rather than Confucian ethical systems) was Japan, which did not really have an examination system during the Tokugawa period.

In the Meiji period, as Japan began modernization and introduced examinations, the number of officials selected was very small. When Tokyo University was established, it was also quite small, and anyone who got into the university not only became an official, but efforts were made to ensure that the students did become officials and did not take some alternate occupation. This was a very tight, elite group, which set very high standards. Accordingly, the entrance examination to Tokyo University became very important. Once this happened, and once they set up eight regional school districts that would have advanced high schools requiring entrance examinations, students were selected in a meritocratic way. This system implies a close link between education and government service, something that is not completely obvious in the United States. Here, higher education is thought of as being for many purposes, originally for the ministry, and not necessarily for government service. The elite institutions in all the East Asian countries have been public institutions that select out a group and thereby define what education brings. One could argue, Vogel believes, that what happened was the rapid expansion of this system to the entire population. In the early Meiji period only a very small group of people could consider passing these examinations. As educational standards went up after World War II, competition became much more intense, and in a sense, everybody who felt that the way to succeed in society was through education now felt that because they were getting higher education they deserved some higher prestige. So the demand for those higher positions was really extraordinary.

Among the consequences of the examination system (as Rohlen discusses) were the key part they played in maintaining discipline in the lower school levels and in bringing all the schools up to very high standards. Of course, in Japan, due to permanent employment, there was a special intensity to pursuit of examination success, since the one critical opportunity for mobility in life was as a teenager when entering the university, leading to getting a good job in a large company right after graduation. To have such an opportunity one must go to a good university.

In the other countries in East Asia, too, Vogel pointed out, examinations are extremely important, with competition very intense—"examination hell." In Taiwan, Singapore, Hong Kong, South Korea, and now the PRC, examinations are all very important. If one looks for some social institutions in East Asia that are relatively unique and not found in other parts of the world, then the entrance examination would be very high as a candidate. In Korea and Taiwan, modern examinations were introduced by the Japanese during occupation. Although only a tiny proportion of the local youth had a chance to pass those examinations, and the highest positions required the students to go to Japan to take the examinations (in Japanese), still it set the tone in modern subjects that were picked up in Taiwan after 1949 and in Korea after 1960. Although these were introduced somewhat in Syngman Rhee's era, it was really after Pak Chung-hee came to power in 1963 that examinations for officials were codified and became a strict system. Certainly Seoul National University has all the same overtones as Tokyo University, and Taiwan University is also extremely similar. It is interesting that all these places have private universities which lead to private business careers, but if one wants a public career, one had best study at the major public university. This, Vogel feels, has overtones from the Confucian: one studies at the national public university that is open to everybody without the requirement of payment (tuition is so low as to be nominal) and where the elite government officials are selected.

One of the peculiar things about Hong Kong is that it has a British administration where the same kind of spirit and same kind of system have become important. Hong Kong University plays the same role for selecting officials in the Hong Kong government that Tokyo University and Seoul National University play in their respective countries. In Singapore, if anything, the situation is even more extreme: there is meritocracy all the way to the top politicians. There is a collapsing of politics and meritocratic bureaucracy there that is not really known in the other countries in East Asia. All the people selected to become representatives have gone through meritocratic exams. Additionally, every year one hundred students are selected by exam for study abroad in order to enrich the intellectual perspective of future leaders.

In sum, Vogel's impression is that this examination culture is extremely important and is common to all parts of East Asia. This includes mainland China, where exams have been employed since 1977; they have moved from, in Susan Shirk's term, "virtuocratic" to meritocratic, from politics in command to qualifications in command.

Ronald Dore, as well, identified examinations as a very important educational phenomenon and offered two points for further consideration. The first related to the previous day's discussion on competition. This is, he feels, a good field for linguistic analysis since the normal word for "competition" in Japan involves the category of "conflict." Traditionally, competition to be selected for the examination system in China was not spoken of in the same terms. Rather, the Chinese term *keju (k'echu,* Jap. *kakyoo)* involves the notion of people being selected and raised. This relates to the role of public authority and the role of the market in economic development and is cognate with a distinction that the American sociologist Turner drew between mobility in American society and that in British society, expressed as a difference between "contest mobility" and "sponsored mobility." The mobility that comes through the educational system is sponsored mobility; in the end, it is not the relative strengths of the competitors that is determinate, but rather the choice made by public authority.

Second, concerning how distinctive the post-Confucian sphere is in its examination system, Dore said that the closest analogies in social systems are to be found in Eastern Europe. It is this kind of system which has produced Gorbachev.

Finally, introducing the life of the Japanese physicist Nagaoka Hanka (fl. ca. 1900), who had been deeply influenced by Confucian thought, Dore noted that for people of his day, Confucianism was not seen as "individual suppressant" and that it was a game that everybody could play provided that they had mastered the basic principles that were to be applied. Also, it involved a certain hubris that was not right-asserting hubris, but rather the attempted exercise of youthful moral authority over what are perceived as corrupt and compromising seniors. One of the essential preconditions for Nagaoka to feel that way about Confucian studies in the 1880s, Dore believes, was that the people who engaged in this kind of argument saw themselves as a meritocratic elite, not as a hereditary property elite. There is a different kind of legitimacy that attaches to people who acquire their elite status through educational performance rather than the inheritance of property, and this is a common feature of the modern-day regimes in East Asia. A further point concerning Nagaoka is how important intellectual achievement seemed to him for national identity. He did not wish merely to be a lackey transmitter of Westerners' ideas. One cannot discuss Confucianism from the middle of the nineteenth century onward without seeing the element of national assertion and the sense of competition between people in the Confucian tradition and Westerners.

Finally, Dore noted that what Nagaoka wanted out of education was some sort of moral satisfaction and not just a ticket to a career. Study just for fame and profit was a danger traditionally warned of within the Confucian tradition.

The awareness of this has given the education received in Japan (and likely the other countries in East Asia, as well) a special quality, Dore feels, even in primary school, that is lacking in, say, the modern schools of Africa, where this tradition is totally lacking and where the primary definition of schools is a place where one gets the certificates to get ahead. But how does one actually define this moral emphasis? Dore wondered if it could not be put this way: If you can range individuals on a dimension, at one end are those who see life as primarily about individual satisfaction, and at the other end are people who see the purpose of human life as primarily the fulfillment of some kind of God-given, family-given, outside-given, transcendently given duty. If people could be ranked along this dimension, Dore feels that it is a reasonable hypothesis that the people in East Asia would cluster more towards the fulfillment of duty end, while those of North America would cluster more towards the individual satisfaction end. Though, of course, this is changing over time. If one were to go to mid-nineteenth-century England, one would likely find the population shifted a good deal further towards the duty end than today.

Dore then asked: What is the role of the education system in producing such an effect? One useful way of answering this question, he believes, is to start by listing a set of functions that are performed in all societies. Thus, all societies have some means of dealing with the trauma of death; they have some means of psychologically dealing with the hazards of everyday life, the possibility of earthquakes; and some means of providing rituals of social solidarity. In Japan, for example, it was the Buddhist rituals that dealt with death, while it was at various Shinto shrines that one prayed to deal with the various hazards of everyday life. These Shinto shrines also provided the focus and idiom for rituals of social solidarity at the community level, while ancestor worship, absorbed into Buddhism from Confucian tradition, provided social solidarity for the family. In other parts of East Asia, the distribution is very different.

Other functions that all societies perform are: first, transmitting intellectual cultures—beliefs about the history of the people, value systems, and so forth; second, transmitting skills, mental and manual; and third, instilling moral norms. In European societies, the division of functions has generally been that where there are schools they do a bit of the cultural transmission, they take care of all the skills transmission, but it is the churches that do the inculcation of moral norms. In Japan, certainly, as most probably in other East Asian societies, as well, the school has performed all three functions. The explicitly religious organizations, which perform the social solidarity rituals and those dealing with death and so forth, have had very little to do with the transmission and maintenance of moral norms. The fact that the functions that post-Christian European societies give to churches and take away from the schools are in Japan given to the schools has been a crucial factor in giving a moral dimension to the whole of the educational process. The role of the ethics classes in Japanese schools has been identified as extremely important in the diffusion of the elite norms to the Japanese populace over the last century. However, nobody much has looked at the democratic revamping of the ethics texts in Japan over the last twenty to thirty years. It would be interesting, Dore feels, to examine the compromise that is reached between, on the one hand, the prewar ideal elite morals, which were exclusively individualistic, and, on the other hand, the rather more solidaristic and communitarian version seen in the postwar period.

Tu Weiming noted that de Bary has been involved in an investigation of how the core values of the spiritual tradition of Confucianism were transmitted in China, Korea, and Japan. For centuries, the content of the educational system there was very much focused on the Four Books, along with Zhu Xi's commentaries, and every educated male adult was exposed very intensively to that form of education. We know that Zhu Xi divided the Four Books into four stages with a specific sequence. One begins with the *Great Learning*. What one gets out of it, Tu feels, is a holistic vision of linking the self, the family, the community, and the state. Underlying this vision is the assumption of the inseparability of moral character, on the one hand, and political leadership, on the other, that is, the whole question of morality and politics. It is understood in terms of the dichotomy (which should not be taken to be necessarily exclusive) of inner and outer: the quest for inner spiritual self-transformation, on the one hand, and public service, on the other. The whole question of moral authority informs both political leadership and personal worth.

Next one moves on to the *Analects*. Tu feels that this work comprises a series of commonsensical notions about how to learn to be human. Following upon Madsen's discussion on the previous day, he observed that the rationality that is implied in the whole discussion is not instrumental rationality, but rather communicative rationality, very much understood as reasonableness. What is meant by reasonable? Very much in keeping with Habermas's notion of the communicative rationality in the life sphere: a sense of reasonableness.

Next comes *Mencius*. What we have there is the Mencian vision, the self-understanding of the intellectual. There is a real hubris of duty. One can even look at Mencius as an apologia for the intellectual as the master of the culture, and therefore the basis of moral authority.

Finally there is the *Doctrine of the Mean*, which represents, Tu said, an attempt to provide inner resources; it deals with questions of sincerity and authenticity and is very much related to the whole question of self-cultivation that Yamashita and Kalton spoke of.

Tu pointed out that the mottos of the Donglin Academy were featured very prominently in modern Chinese political culture, for example, during the early period of the Cultural Revolution with Wu Han, the student demonstration of April 5, 1976, and again in recent months. These mottos are simply these:

> The sound of the wind, the sound of the rain, and the sound of the recitation of the classics: each sound enters into my ear *(fengsheng yusheng dushusheng shengsheng ruer)*.

> The affairs of the family, the affairs of the nation, and the affairs all under heaven, each affair is our personal concern *(jiashi guoshi tianxiasi shishi guanxin)*.

This sense of the educated person as responsible, not only for private affairs, but also those of the state, this sort of hubris, is very powerful. Even though for seventy years now in China (and likely also in Korea and Japan) very few people have been exposed to the Four Books in the same way provided by traditional education, yet if one looks at the ethical texts in Japan, Korea, Taiwan, or for that matter in the PRC, one finds the particular ethos of the inseparability of politics and morality, on the one hand, and the idea of the person as a center of relationships in a much larger network, on the other, together with an emphasis on duty consciousness over rights consciousness. These remnants are very pervasive. So the core curriculum consciously designed by some of the neo-Confucian masters not only dominated East Asian education for centuries, but also has continued to have these repercussions.

De Vos raised a question concerning the educational system related to mentorship. The discussion so far had stressed the examination system seen as, perhaps, a bit of a mass production. In Japan's *iemoto* system, people would be brought in and tutored by particular individuals. In the Chinese case, both traditionally and in modern times, how did mentorship interact within the examination system, that is, how did one learn from someone as part of self-development?

Henry Rosovsky added to this question by asking why the examination system is not a weakness, rather than a strength of the system, since clearly people are not equal in their ability to take these examinations, and certain groups have advantages. In contrast, the American system takes account of many different qualities, and one could argue that this produces a fairer result.

Vogel responded by noting that it has not been easy in any of the East Asian societies to make the transition to a modern, meritocratic society. By being very strict about the examinations, there is absolute legitimation. For example, in Japan, if one used recommendations as an important criterion, people would not give the same detached recommendations that we in the West try to. In order both to have legitimacy in society and to provide for meritocracy, Vogel believes that the examination system is unassailable. Once the examination is passed, then, of course, personal qualities become important. On the question raised by De Vos, Vogel said that in modern-day Taiwan, Singapore, and mainland China there is no longer individual mentorship, but rather group *peiyang* (cultivation). This includes training and moral education. In Taiwan, for example, at the higher level of officialdom, the Guomindang has selected about thirty people a year to go to Yangming Mountain for special training; on the mainland, the Party school (the *dangxiao*) has much the same quality. So, it is not so much the old mentor relationship, but instead group selection done by organizations. However, there still is much added quality involving morality, a sense of responsibility, and group loyalty.

Tu Weiming offered one qualification to Vogel's remarks. That is, in graduate education, as it has been reinstituted in China, mentorship still seems to be the norm. It has been institutionalized in that a graduate student in a major university studying, say, humanities or social sciences is a part of a team following a master. The Educational Commission will not grant authority to any institution to train doctoral students. Rather, they only identify specific scholars—for example, Feng Youlan—who are given permission to train doctoral students in whatever institution he is associated with. In the field of, say, the history of Chinese philosophy only about ten to fifteen receive this special designation: these people will be the masters in training a whole generation of scholars in this area. In China, there is currently a problem with the generation gap between teachers and students. When students become dissatisfied with their mentors it creates many problems. Even in Taiwan, if not within the university system, sometimes outside it, mentorship is important. This is especially the case in Buddhist, Taoist, and Confucian studies. In fact, Tu noted, a number of Western academics have been beneficiaries of this system. For example, there is one master, Liu Yuyun (Liu Yu-yun), who teaches Chinese classics with an emphasis on Confucianism. Scholars such as Frederick Wakeman, Nathan Sivin, Peter Bol, and others are all his disciples. If you look at who's who in Chinese intellectual history, a significant percentage studied with him.

Peter Bol, on the issue of examinations, observed that it was important to remember that an examination education has been consistently criticized in the past by all major intellectual movements. Zhu Xi, and other Song neo-Confucianists, railed against examination education. When the Four Books got co-opted and put into examination education there were private academies that strongly criticized such education. In the Qing dynasty, when the evidential learning movement appeared, their academies also attacked examination education. Now, it is certainly true that public is better than private in education in China. Yet, at the same time, public education there—and perhaps in East Asia in general—today has far more clout than it did in the past, when more schools were private, and these were more seriously engaged in training and teaching than the public ones. On the question of mentorship, private academies in the past served to a far greater extent than the public schools (though this was not always the case) as centers of advanced learning and intellectual creativity. It is in this setting, in the private academy, that the teacher becomes an intellectual sponsor.

Dore said that it was important to point out that although everyone in Japan who has a child going through the education system assumes it is the brain one is born with that is ultimately going to determine success in the examinations, the whole rhetoric of the system concentrates on effort. The assumption is that the people who do well are those who study hardest. The reward then becomes a reward for effort of will, which is under the control of an individual, not in the genes.

A second point brought up by Dore related to efficiency: styles of authority in organization are relevant. In Britain, for example, authority is always problematic, and a rights-asserting population is always likely to challenge a manager. Accordingly, the personality requirements for occupying general managerial positions there are rather more important than in Japan, where authority is much less commonly problematic. Dore is uncertain whether this is the result of the survival of deference, or differing traditions of styles of authority, or a difference in the quality of interpersonal relationships in general. But certainly the success of Japanese managers with British and American workers does suggest that styles of management may be responsible. The point is, Dore maintained, that because the power to overawe people, the power to get people to do what you want by sheer force of personality, is a less-important requirement for people in top management, brains and the ability to solve problems intellectually can become more important criteria. So the efficiency cost of using that as the main selector item when selecting people for jobs in top corporations is less than in the West.

Richard Madsen said that another point to consider is the way in which different Asian societies resolve the potential tension between admission to higher education on the basis of merit and the acquisition of a job on the basis of some connection through mentorship. In mainland China, one of the primary grievances of the students is that although now a meritocratic system allows them entrance into universities, getting any sort of job after that depends upon connections *(guanxi)*. In societies where that tension is not quite so stark, there may be a happier resolution to this issue.

Chang Hao, addressing a point made by Bol, reminded him that private academies became unimportant after the seventeenth century, because the Manchu government imposed a ban on such academies. They still existed, but only in the form that is meant to be preparatory for the examination system. They, therefore, no longer performed the same function they had prior to the seventeenth century. Therefore, after the seventeenth century the center of education moved back to the private system within either a single wealthy family or that of a group of families pooling their resources.

Bol responded by noting that in the eighteenth century the government relaxed the prohibition of private academies. It is true that there was a great deal of state involvement in them, but they were not necessarily examination training centers: look at the *xuehaitang* in Canton.

Chang also addressed Rosovsky's earlier question about whether the examination system was fair. As Bol said earlier, from the Confucian point of view of the moral development of the individual, the examination system could be a diversion, especially after the advent of the Ming dynasty, that is, from the fourteenth–fifteenth centuries, when the main subject tested was a formalistic essay with no content whatsoever. In other words, one of the charges leveled against the examination system was that it did not really test people's moral quality, but rather that it merely tested their ability to do rote learning. In the late nineteenth century and the modern period, the charge leveled against the examination system was based on the feeling that the tests were empty of the practical content necessary to run the government. Accordingly, many people in China have felt that the examination system is a liability rather than a triumph, even though theoretically it is a very good idea, promoting as it does a meritocratic society.

Michael Kalton said that any investigation of the institutional history of the examination system would need to look very carefully at the question of whether the present system really is a Japanese creation, rather than an outgrowth of something Confucian. Certainly in the Korean tradition the private academy tradition looms very large. At the high point, in the eighteenth century, there were more than six hundred private academies. These served as diverse power bases that divided the power within the bureaucracy itself and kept any kind of total centralization of the system away from the monarchy. So, the Confucian academies did not serve as a focal control point in the same way as may be imagined in some other systems.

The structuring of this whole arrangement by the Japanese has been, Kalton asserted, immensely successful. This relates to some of our questions regarding fairness and competition in the exam system. One raw material being focused on in this system, but hitherto not mentioned, is the Confucian bond between classmates, which is immensely strong wherever the institution is. In Korea one notable example is the various military coups by colonels. These have been engineered by single classes from the military academy; everyone goes up and goes down together. This phenomenon also is widely visible in civilian life in corporate hiring practices and so forth. The structuring of the significance of this extremely strong relationship among people into a hierarchy of recognized institutions and recognized worth is, Kalton believes, very important in the modern system. In Korea it serves to legitimize in a public way what would otherwise be a competitive situation seen to be based on arbitrary preferences and relationships.

Gilbert Rozman said that this last theme tied into reactions he had to several comments, namely, the theme of legitimation and how to satisfy public opinion or the opinion of people in organizations. The combination of religion, education, and political mobility relates to this focus on legitimation. We can look at this at several points in time. Vogel brought up the Japanese success in coming up in the 1880s with a new system. The decline of Confucianism, Rozman believes, was much tempered and kept within bounds—so that Confucian values did not become a negative symbol the way they did in China—in part by the speed of the decline and the quick replacement with a new system of legitimating through education the new relationship between the political elite and the masses. At this point in history, Rozman feels, there is a new problem of legitimation in both countries with no obvious solution. In China this problem is more pronounced, and it relates to the failure to satisfy the intellectuals, even after the reinstatement of the exam system. As Madsen brought out earlier, there has been no link-up with elite status. Also, moral education has faded in the 1980s, so that there is no clear sense of how this new system is legitimate. There is, Rozman observed, a possibility of legitimation through socialism, but the leadership has failed to do what is necessary. The same thing occurs on a lesser scale in Japan today, where also no new leadership is in sight and there is much dissatisfaction. This is not just the result of corruption, although that is important, but involves also the educational system and a sense of decline in confidence in the system and in the moral education related to it, and in the ability of the intellectuals to establish an adequate life for themselves because of increasing housing prices.

Samuel Yamashita said that he was still struggling with the question of the transmission of Confucian values and whether in fact they are transmitted. He was struck by the fact that in the case of Japan the emphasis on effort is interesting: one might argue that there is a language of effort, and that if one deconstructs this, one finds that there are Confucian elements, Shinto elements, and Buddhist elements. It is very difficult to track these. Perhaps there are several different paradigms of praxis operating. In some instances they may be more Confucian, while in others they may owe more to the warrior tradition. Or there may be a synthetic paradigm in which the elements have become fused.

Yamashita also noted that he was struck by the amount of continuity with respect to the language of effort. He gave the example of a famous diary kept by a schoolgirl during World War II in which she talks about being evacuated and life in the country. It is interesting that the language she uses is the language of effort, quite similar to that being used now.

A further point is that another important nexus to be considered is: For whom is one studying as one sits for an exam? Is one doing it for self? For family? This really has not been discussed so far.

Woody Watson, following up on the question of what is Confucian in education and what stems from other elements, noted that, at least in the Chinese context, if one looks at the local level, it is at the primary school where one can begin to distinguish "genuine" Confucian elements as opposed to other elements of popular culture. Even up to the 1960s, among the Canton refugees in Hong Kong whom Watson was studying, many boys attended lineage schools taught in the ancestral hall, literally under the eyes of their ancestors, whose tablets were on the wall; their education involved, essentially, the chanting of Confucian texts. Watson would interpret this as the result of an effort on the part of local elites to impose some notion of cultural hegemony at that level. However, in every other aspect of peasant life, Confucianism rarely reared its head, rarely had any presence at all. Certainly, after the students left the school, their lives were taken over by popular culture. But during this formative period, virtually all the men who learned how to read, at least at the elementary level, had some experience of Confucianism.

MacFarquhar asked why the local elites wished to instill it.

Watson said he believes they wished to represent their own culture as being acceptable. It was in the vested interests of local elites to present themselves as acceptable to imperial authorities and other state authorities. For not to do so would have made them the targets of punitive raiding. So it was in the interests of the local elites to maintain some sort of control over the local schools. It was interesting that the ability of all the men who had a minimal level of literacy (meaning that they could more or less read a newspaper or bus schedules) was based on a Confucian textual tradition. Accordingly, Watson would look to primary education as being more critical in understanding Confucian elements in local Chinese society.

Tu Weiming said that if a distinction is made between cultural sophistication and level of literacy, then the situation becomes quite interesting. Traditionally, the real cultural transmitter early in the lives of young boys was the mother. The role of educator was really assumed by the mothers, who were often not literate, but were culturally sophisticated. One out of many examples is that of a mother in the seventeenth century who told her son, "I would like you to learn from the two fatherless gentlemen in ancient China: one was Confucius, whose father died when Confucius was three, and the other was Mencius. Recently general surveys of biographies of major thinkers in the Confucian tradition starting from the fourteenth century have shown that the overwhelming majority, including Wang Yangming, were trained in the formative years by their mothers through oral transmission.

Watson said that this was extremely interesting, but wondered how much of such stories were mythological representations taken from Mencius or other texts. He noted that he had heard them many times and felt that it was an interesting cultural depiction. Howerever, he would question how rooted it was in the culture versus the traditional scholar-bureaucratic representation of society.

De Vos responded to Watson's and Tu's comments, noting that they had addressed themes he would be himself taking up in a subsequent presentation, which he had tentatively titled "The pleasures of propriety," or alternatively, "The morality of propriety." This, he felt, starts in the body. Also, rote learning is often quite misunderstood. Such learning begins at quite a young age and is not, De Vos argues, rote learning as such, but rather the ritual of reading and reading as ritual. If we look at ritual and see what is ritual in Confucianism, there is a secret there. It is here that it becomes, in a sense, religious. The analogy in the West is the Jewish tradition, in which scholarship is also ritualized to a certain degree. This dimension is also part of the Confucian tradition. It involves how ritual is used in the concept of self-development. He said that he would elaborate on these themes in the next session.

Dore, on the general topic of democratization in Confucian society and the problem of legitimation, said that in Japan the politicians distinguish themselves from all other elite groups in not being selected through an entrance examination. Baseball stars, television personalities, and politicians are the only three kinds of elites that do not depend on the examination system. We see a process of hereditary transmission setting in in the Liberal-Democratic Party in Japan: something like 40 percent of all LDP lower house members are the sons or nephews of LDP members. This is also *the* main item of corruption in the Japanese system. It seems a bit different from what is happening in Korea and China. There, the students are behaving like the junior members in an elite organization, attacking their superiors for moral failures. On the other hand, the criticisms directed at politicians in Japan are of a quite different order and are directed by the relatively clean examination-performance-legitimated bureaucracies against that island of what is becoming increasingly hereditary corruption. The more Korea democratizes and the more China develops representative organs on similar lines, the more there will be this strange enclave, which calls for a different kind of legitimation.

MacFarquhar said that Dore's earlier remarks on how the British in the nineteenth century were more on the duty end of the spectrum had reminded him that at the private school he had attended there were on the wall of the chapel the last words of a headmaster who had died, literally with his boots on while in office, to the effect that "Duty is the only thing worth living for." He suggested an analogy as a way of gaining a perspective on the kind of problems being discussed. In a sense, what the United Kingdom did in the nineteenth century was to create a Confucian system for a brief while, in the sense that, instead of pursuing a modernizing role, the aristocracy managed to divert the incoming elite into an imperial role and to instill the concept of duty, which permeated the class. Because of the success of the imperial enterprise, it filtered down sufficiently for everyone to get behind the act. By the end of the Second World War, there was an increasing demand for rights on the part of the working class. One of problems of British society today is that the duty consciousness of the middle class breaks down as it sees the working-class demands for rights resulting in getting rights and questioning why they themselves should not do the same.

MacFarquhar further argues that a similar breakdown took place in China during the Cultural Revolution; that the authority of the Communist Party was eroded by the chairman himself; and that what we have here is an administration that is still clinging to the idea of duty—that is its gospel. Marxism-Leninism does not have nearly the same educative force, so the notion of "socialist spiritual civilization," which is totally meaningless, has no impact whatsoever. On the other hand is the demand for rights, which is being articulated at the moment by students and others: there is a conflict between duty and rights in China. It is interesting to look at Japan, where, despite total defeat, occupation, and democratization, the demand for rights appears to be singularly absent, at least when compared with Korea, Taiwan, and China.

Political Culture and Economic Ethics

HENRY ROSOVSKY CALLED on Tu Weiming to open by introducing the topic.

Tu said that when we speak of "Confucian humanism" we often assume that it is intertwined with a particular form of economy, namely, an agriculture-based economy with a family-centered social structure and a polity with a paternalistic central bureaucracy as its salient feature. This is, Tu feels, one of the reasons why Lucian Pye, for example, in his general discussion of the spirit of Chinese politics and the nature of power and authority in East Asia, puts a great deal of emphasis on Confucian political culture as centered on the whole question of authority. Some would say a form of authoritarianism. This is also the reason, Tu continued, why some people believe that once a society moves out of an agriculture-based economy, that society is relatively de-Confucianized. That is also the reason that many people put so much emphasis on Confucian ethics as a form of family ethics.

The intriguing problem for the last forty years or so has been to ask whether Confucian ethics or Confucian humanism is really wedded to an agriculture-based economy or even a kind of conservative mentality of an agriculture-based economy that is not able to transform into an industrial-based economy, and whether that particular kind of political culture is so much a reflection of the authoritarian mechanism of control that it is by definition incompatible with democratization. Tu's own feeling is that the situation is much more complicated. The question of how profit is understood, the question of economic planning, whether it is short-term or long-term, is also relevant here. In an aside, Tu noted that when we examine some of the so-called insights in the economic arena, either in the *Analects* or in *Mencius* or some other texts, usually the point is made that unless the livelihood of the people is sustained, unless there is sufficient prosperity, it is not possible to develop a moral community. There is obvious emphasis on the importance of wealth. But not wealth for its own sake. Hence, there is a conflict between wealth and power, on the one hand, and moral community, on the other. But the conflict is sometimes resolved in traditional society by directing profit-making energy toward a larger goal—in a cynical way, some kind of pretext, some kind of justification for a particular behavior. So if we look at the social-political dynamics of East Asia today, the language of Confucian discourse (as Sam Yamashita has discussed) may have undergone some variety of transformation. These are some of the issues that might be addressed.

Carter Eckert said that he had been quite excited by the prospect of the workshop until he got a schedule and learned that he was to be one of the speakers!

He began by returning to one of the *problematiques* of the previous day: the issue of the pursuit of profit. One of the essential structural features of capitalism, Eckert believes, is, regardless of the culture, an intense personal interest in the pursuit of profit on the part of the people who are most involved, for example, the businessmen, capitalists, entrepreneurs, and so forth. Someone, perhaps Freud, once said that intellectuals are people who have discovered something more interesting than sex. One might say the same thing of businessmen; in their case, the discovery is money rather than ideas. This does not mean necessarily that there are not some other ideological factors involved, such as love of humanity, the nation, whatever. Yet it seems that the all-consuming passion is capital accumulation for its own sake. And it would also seem that if one's real passion is love of humanity or the nation, then there are other occupations that are perhaps more suitable than running a big company. Eckert stressed that he was not trying to be judgmental about economics or capitalism. Rather he feels that these views have a basis in logic and also in empirical evidence. In the course of his work on Korean capitalism, he had many occasions to meet Korean businessmen, got to know some of them quite well personally, and also sat in on a number of strategy sessions in companies, and even in some of the board of directors meetings. In the closed-door, private atmosphere, the discussion always centered on the bottom line: making money. Keynes put it very well when he said that the essential characteristic of capitalism is an intense appeal to the money-making instinct of individuals.

There is a problem with this, one not necessarily an East Asian one: avarice has never been one of the cardinal virtues either in the West or the East. So capitalist societies (or would-be capitalist societies) have had to adjust, or somehow transform, the traditional morality in order to accommodate this pursuit-of-profit ethos. The solution to the problem in the West has been centered on the idea of the market, Adam Smith's famous invisible hand. In many ways, Eckert feels, this was an ingenious solution—in spite of the fact that it stirred up a whole host of dissenters, of whom Karl Marx was the most notable—and one that has been enduring, especially in the United States. For the capitalist class, the market places no moral onus on the pursuit of profit. People can be as greedy as they like and still feel good about it because through the market mechanism this greed is serving a larger and public purpose. Also if we consider the means through which people pursue profit, it is a comfortable idea for the capitalist class. As long as one does not violate any laws (and it is important to keep in mind that the legal system is more or less biased in favor of the market in the United States), one is relatively free to pursue profit, by whatever means he or she chooses.

Another issue is the final ends or result. The idea of the market is again comfortable for the capitalists, the Smithean idea being that the pursuit of individual property is supposed to produce public as well as private wealth. But if it doesn't, if, for example, there is a depression, or whatever, the capitalist can claim that it really is not his or her fault, that it really is a problem of market distortions, such as government interference.

On the whole, Eckert feels that though it is a huge generalization, the market ideas formulated by Smith in the West have been a fairly happy solution to this problem of the pursuit of profit. They have helped to release the energies of the capitalist class and also produced a fairly strong legitimation for capitalism in the West, especially in the United States.

In Korea and Japan (and presumably in China as well) the story has been somewhat different. In Korea capitalism was an imported idea before it became a class or an economic system. The people who provided the Korean solution to the pursuit-of-profit problem were literati who were more or less enmeshed in a world very different from that of the Western capitalists, one dominated by Confucian and nationalist ideas. The solution turned out to be much more restrictive for the capitalist class than in the West.

The first person to deal with this in Korea was a scholar-bureaucrat named Yu Kil-chun, who wrote in the 1880s. He started out by making a point of criticizing the traditional view of merchants as having very low status in society and went so far as to call them heroes. This was quite a departure from the traditional view. But he also laid down some restrictions regarding motivations, means, and ends. The hero-merchant must be motivated not by a desire for personal profit, but by a desire to make comfortable the living conditions of the people, on the one hand, and also to keep the state strong and independent, on the other. In other words, you can pursue profit, but not for the sake of profit. You can do it for the love of humanity and for the nation, but not for the sake of profit itself. In connection with the means, Yu stressed the importance of the merchants' making it on their own, with no special favors from the government, and on the basis of trust and sincerity in dealing with other people, a sense of right and wrong, and also the cultivation of proper skills and knowledge that are appropriate to the merchant, such as bookkeeping. In terms of the final ends or results, Yu argued very strongly that the merchant was personally responsible for the achievement of these goals, that is, making the life of the people easier and keeping the state strong and independent. If these goals are not being achieved, he suggests that blame lies very strongly with the merchants for not acting properly and for seeking personal profit at the expense of public good, for not being sincere or righteous, or not learning the proper skills. This view has come to dominate the mainstream discourse on capitalism in Korea. Even businessmen themselves have adopted it more or less wholesale as an official ideology. So one can find numerous quotations such as the following passage from the biography of a very well-known Korean businessman, Kim Yong-won.

> As Korea developed into a highly industrialized society in the midst of adverse domestic and international conditions, Kim Yong-won devoted himself to guarding against the excessive selfishness that came in the wake of industrialization and concentrated all his efforts on seeing that business profits were properly returned to society. Like Kim Song-su and Kim Yon-su, who never used business profits for their own personal ends and pleasure, Kim Yong-won based his behavior and daily life on the principles of frugality and moderation. Thoroughly imbued with a spirit of public service, he always put the welfare of the nation above personal gain and prestige.

This sort of language is typical, Eckert noted, of passages one encounters in the memoirs of businessmen, biographies, autobiographies, and company histories.

In conclusion, Eckert commented on the positive and negative aspects of this Korean solution to the problem of profit. There are also many correspondences to these in Japan. The positive side has been the promotion of economic development. There has been a niche, an important one in fact, reserved for capitalist activity in the economy. At the same time, the Korean solution has kept businessmen more or less subordinate to state interests. Although this is becoming something of a problem now, as the Korean economy has expanded and become very complex, in the early stages this was very much a positive aspect, where state-directed economic development was essential.

The less positive side of this, Eckert said, has to do with the question of social and political stability. The South Korean *chaebol* are very widely regarded as having violated all three aspects of their own adopted ideology. First of all, few, including the businessmen themselves, seem to believe that the big businessmen have been motivated by love of humanity and the nation. In fact, this is a major political weakness of the orthodox capitalist view in Korea, the fact that it refuses to acknowledge profit for its own sake as morally acceptable. Second, the whole process of capital accumulation in South Korea, and also going back before 1945, has taken place through the filter of the state, often in a context of special favors and corruption. Not, in other words, primarily through the independent efforts of the entrepreneurs themselves.

The third matter is that of equity and economic nationalism, which are two things that one hears much of today in South Korea, both in mainstream and also in more radical critiques of society. The economic development process has been skewed towards class interests (that of the larger businessmen), on the one hand, and also regional interests, on the other. Development has tended to follow a Seoul–Pusan axis, resulting in development of the southeast while grossly ignoring the southwest, the Cholla provinces, from which many of the opposition political figures have come. In terms of sales, in 1985 the top five businesses accounted for nearly 66 percent of GNP in terms of sales and about 12 percent of value added. These figures have been growing steadily since the 1960s. There is also much concern in South Korea over the structural dependence of the national economy on the U.S. market and on Japanese technology. The Hyundai car is an interesting example. The engine comes from Mitsubishi, and many of the key components are also imported from Japan. As sales were booming for the Hyundai in the United States, the Koreans were having to run up a huge trade deficit with Japan at the same time. This has become a political issue in South Korea and is providing fairly strong fuel for a growing critique of the capitalist system there, one that has taken on, among a minority, a kind of revolutionary position seeking to dismantle the *chaebol* and really transform the social-economic system.

Thus, in sum, this Confucian-nationalist view of capitalism in South Korea has been economically productive, but it also has raised some interesting and important questions about the political stability of the capitalist system itself.

Rosovsky first noted, in response to Eckert's presentation, that when Japan was in a certain sense "more Confucian" (if one can say that) than it has been since the Meiji Restoration, that is, during the Tokugawa era, one of the great problems was that the authorities could not conceive of the merchants as being productive. They viewed them in a physiocratic sense. Now a big change has taken place, and everything Eckert spoke of was close to the Japanese situation. How this change occurred he is not sure.

Rosovsky spoke of his interest in an issue that has long been debated in discussing Japanese economic development. Before World War II there was much talk in Japan about its beautiful customs, about the connection between more modern Japanese economic institutions and the historical premodern background of the country. In some ways, this view has been pushed aside entirely by an assault coming particularly from within Japan, but foreigners in recent years have criticized the beautiful-customs view that is identified with works such as Jim Abegglen's book, *The Japanese Factory*. More and more the view has come about that, in fact, what is unusual about Japanese economic structure, particularly labor relations (permanent employment, etc.) is really the consequence of objective economic circumstances relating to Japan's late start or comparative backwardness. Rosovsky believes that people have gone much too far over to one side and that as he looks at Japanese economic development he sees a whole host of things that can be traced quite directly to pre-Meiji times, and therefore presumably to a value system that has very little to do with the introduction of the West or the specific situation in which Japan found itself in the 1860s, that is, the necessity of catch-up.

Next Rosovsky gave seven factors that he has identified.

1. Long-run orientation
2. Emphasis on saving and thrift
3. Concern with quality
4. Suspicion of foreigners
5. Emphasis on knowing markets
6. Exploiting indigenous strengths
7. A certain desire for regulation, order, guidance; or from an economic point of view, the desire to avoid excessive competition.

These orientations come from a work Rosovsky views as one of the most extraordinary documents in modern Japanese economic history, the *Kogyo iken* (usually translated as *A Survey of Industries*), published in 1884 by the Ministry of Agriculture and Commerce. To summarize briefly, the Japanese published in 1884 a thirty-volume development plan, the first development plan of any country known to Rosovsky, a plan that contains not only discussion of what the next century was to be like, but also, and more important, a plan that contains ten-year targets, quite specific in many instances, most of which were in fact accomplished. For example, these ten-year targets go from rather general principles, such as making Japan strong, to seventy-five specific recommendations, such as establishing silk inspection stations at Yokohama, tea inspection stations at Yokohama and Kobe, the constant leit-motif of quality. In *Kogyo iken* the seven points listed above come up again and again, and Rosovsky finds it quite clear that they could not have simply been invented out of nothing, but instead that they go back to a tradition, to a value system, with, perhaps, certain Confucian predilections.

Here is an illustrative passage on savings and the desire for order:

Should we content ourselves with a life in which we are able only to pay back our own debts? We must not let ourselves be satisfied with such a level of life. Only when a man contemplates his future can he be considered a true human being. If he spends all his earnings, leaving nothing for savings, his life is no different from that of an animal. We cannot always be young and active so we must prepare for our old age. If we have children, we must increase our property so that it can be divided among them. If we are merely concerned with protecting property inherited from forefathers, and do not increase our property beyond the amount we have inherited, how can we advance the welfare of our society. Our forefathers worked hard for us and we also have to strive for a better life for our children. We can regard savings as the duty of our life.

Still on savings, and incredible when one considers life in the United States in the 1980s:

There are three types of economies. The best type is the one that creates revenue that is larger than expenditures and thus increases the surplus after meeting all necessary expenses. The next best type maintains a balance between revenue and expenditure. The worst type is deficit financing in which expenditures exceed revenue. Take a look at both the economy of our government and the economy of the people. In which type of economy are we living? In order to finance our imports we have used up all our gold and silver accumulated in the past. If we fail now to curb our expenses from unproductive undertakings and if we do not pursue productive undertakings more directly, we will be forced to rely on unmined gold and silver in the future. Obviously, the government's generous policy of reducing the land tax by one-sixth [in the early 1880s] misled the people. They began to want luxuries instead of saving their money. The government also established a private ownership system of land by issuing title deeds to individual persons. However, the result was regrettably contrary to the government's intention. There is evidence that farmers sold land and abandoned the inherited occupation of farmer, eventually losing all property. Considering this situation, we cannot help but say that if the government handles ignorant people by means of generous policies, it will only result in the weakening of the nation's economic power and the worsening of the people's economic condition.

One more passage about order:

After the restoration every effort was made to remove traditional feudal barriers and practices, which had hindered free entry into trade. In this attempt laws and customs regardless of their merits or demerits were all removed and the people were left free to engage in businesses according to their own choices. If the people had had advanced knowledge and the ability to judge rightly at that time they could have selectively maintained the strong points in the old customs and practices while abandoning the harmful ones, thus enabling them to better manage their enterprises. However, our people have not yet reached that situation. In the beginning they simply followed what the government tried to do, and then the current trend became one of total change, regardless of the value of traditional customs and practices. Eventually the people lost every important custom and practice. In short, the government's policy of lessening its control over the people's economic activity resulted in a chaotic situation among them.

Then it goes on to say what has to be reestablished. It seems clear that this long-term plan, this emphasis on a decade and even beyond goes very deeply into the Japanese psyche. And brought to the process of meeting the West, it can be said that no other country that had faced the advanced world before Japan approached it in anything like this systematic, planned manner also emphasizing the responsibility of the government and the seven factors mentioned previously.

Eckert said that Rosovsky's comments reminded him of Yu Kil-chun's writings, at least in scope and attempt to analyze similar problems, albeit many of the points are mentioned only in a very tangential way. The difference was that Yu was out of power, or rather, never really got into power.

Rosovsky made a further point: This plan is not just a little essay; it is thirty volumes of virtually every prefecture and region in Japan and includes analysis of what was happening in the rest of the world. It was a very systematic effort, and this makes it particularly interesting.

Samuel Yamashita asked whether there were any European models (Prussian, for example) for this sort of endeavor. Given that the model was a centralized one, his suspicion is that it is derived from elsewhere.

Rosovsky said that, yes, there were models. Prussia is the outstanding case for comparison, but he, while not an expert, does not know of any such plan that was as systematic as this one. The Japanese were, to some extent, acquainted with the European experience. The person most responsible for writing the plan was an official named Maeda Masana, who studied in France for about four years. Matsukata Masayoshi was also involved. Maeda wanted a more state-led solution than was finally adopted. He wanted the Japanese in the 1880s to set up a central development bank where investment funds would go. Matsukata was in favor of selling all state-owned Japanese industries. He felt the government simply could not develop them. He gave much more freedom to private entrepreneurs interacting with government bureaucrats. In fact, Matsukata finally won—no such development bank was created.

Gilbert Rozman said that he felt Rosovsky's remarks indicated a need to examine the Tokugawa system to find explanations for Meiji economic behavior. For example, knowing the markets, the service ethic, the importance of state guidance, and the justification of profits as a service to one's area were all present in the Tokugawa period. Whether these characteristics should be identified as distinctly Tokugawa rather than Confucian is a separate question. Rozman felt that at least some of the characteristics mentioned struck him as distinctly Tokugawa, such as knowing the markets.

Rosovsky responded that he had not put together these features with Confucius in mind, but rather had been interested in the question of what feature of Japanese economic behavior might be seen as going far back into the past. One of the most surprising things in this document for Rosovsky was the Japanese realization in the early 1880s of the advantage of backwardness. In the West this idea first came with Veblen. Then, of course, Gerschenkron made the idea much more popular and never gave credit to Veblen, but both in *Imperial Germany and the Industrial Revolution* and the essay on Japan, Veblen says this very specifically. But he wrote at the turn of the century. Listen to the following from Japan in 1884:

> Britain and France have already developed their agriculture, industry, and commerce to a very advanced stage and so it should be very difficult for them to achieve a comparable rate of development in the next ten years. Agriculture, industry, and commerce in our nation have not yet made such progress and careful observation will disclose the fact that our rates of growth should be much higher than those of more developed countries. Let us explain this point using silk as an example. If we can increase our silk prices to the level of French silk prices it will mean an increase of 20–30% in the present price. On the other hand, it should be difficult for France to increase its silk prices by even 10%.

Such passages, Rosovsky feels, show an extremely sophisticated understanding of the world in which they lived.

Schwartz said that, leaving aside for the moment the word *Confucianism,* and speaking of late traditional Chinese development, he would suggest that East Asian development in this latter period may have helped those countries avoid certain dogmas that the West has fallen into. There was, he feels, a growth in a market economy, in a traditional way, in Ming and Qing China. There was a growth in commodity production, in a traditional way, not attached to the idea of limitless economic growth. But the notion that the market was some sort of closed sphere with which the state could not interfere was not there.

Some scholars speak of the late Qing economy as a command economy. Well, it was not that. But the notion that it could intervene ad hoc whenever it wanted to in the market was certainly there. We have had some theses dealing with Qing China that have emphasized the remarkable growth of commodity production and market economy and some that emphasize rather the opposite, the remarkable way in the which the state continued to intervene. Lilian Lee has suggested that state intervention in famine control was something quite remarkable. A sharp distinction arises out of the notion (and here Schwartz confesses he may be showing his prejudice) that economics can be built into an exact science, namely, that an economy is either a total market economy or a centrally planned economy. What happened in communist China was that one of the Western ideologies, which thought centralized planning was infallible, gained control. Where this did not happen, the notion that there could be a market economy and that the government should not intervene when it was advantageous to do so just did not catch hold. Furthermore, as Weber discussed, a modern industrial economy produces not just a new merchant class or a new entrepreneurial class, but also an industrial bureaucratic class, and someone who is a bureaucrat in industry is not so different from a bureaucrat in government. They do not belong to such disparate worlds. So, in East Asia they did not become captured by these "absolutizations" of something like a pure market economy or a pure state-run economy.

Tu said that one school of thought, in which Chang Hao has been deeply involved, is the *jingshi* or statecraft school, sometimes called *jingji*, or Japanese *keizai*, the modern term in Japan for economics. When the Chinese say *jingji*, they have economics in mind rather than any classical Confucian notion. The term comes from *jingshi jimin*, "to manange the world and help the people." This mode of thought has been very powerful. This is reflected quite clearly, for instance, in the works of the Korean sixteenth-century thinker Yi Yulgok (or Yi I), the leader of the so-called vital energy school.

If one wants to find one general category of Confucians in traditional East Asian society, then it is basically the bureaucrat, the scholar-official. They were very much involved in various kinds of management tactics, whether as a magistrate or a central official. They were very much concerned, not with economic issues in the modern sense of a highly specialized, exact science, but in the classical category of political economy. Those involved in this political economic, *jingshi* enterprise were concerned with managing the world from a long-term perspective. There can be no question about their vision: it was always for more than five or six generations. Also, there is an agricultural mentality involved. Farmers are considered different from merchants because they do generate food. Hence physiocratic notions were very important in informing the importance of saving. Even in modern East Asian societies such as Taiwan, the agriculture mentality is still very important in terms of the leadership. Someone once pointed out that Chiang Ching-guo had visited many farming communities, even though in Taiwan they constitute a very small part of the economy. But he never even visited one factory. Similarly, the current president, Lee Teng-hui, has a Ph.D. in agriculture from Cornell. Also, in Japan, the agricultural communities are politically quite powerful. Then, too, there is a strong sense that the economy involves a continuous process: the sense that you do not create something new, you do not start from scratch, you do not have a blueprint for something that is always futuristic. You have to be accountable to the cumulative social-political processes, and not only for your children, but also for your ancestors. The rules and regulations are indigenous resources governing how this will be accomplished.

One of the central features of this Confucian political economy that continues to be very important is the state, not in our modern understanding as an instrument of political control, but rather the state as an ethical-religious mechanism which, through its leadership, will be able to do much to both develop and order the society. Although these notions are quite interesting, very few scholars working on the Confucian tradition are interested in the statecraft tradition.

Rosovsky suggested a possible topic relevant to Schwartz's and Tu's remarks: How do Confucian ethics specifically affect economic behavior? For example, it seems that Tu is saying that a Confucian could live with state interference; it would be part of the natural order of things. Also (perhaps more rhetorical than behavior) there is the notion of the community-centered entrepreneur spoken of by Eckert and also heard in Japan.

Ezra Vogel noted that one thing striking to him was the difference in economic behaviors in the different countries. This may be partly due to being at different stages of economic growth. For example, in Japan there are now the so-called mature corporations that have been separated for generations from the original owner. In South Korea, basically there are first-generation, very large, owner-run *chaebol* corporations just now beginning the transition to the second generation. In Taiwan there is a plethora of much smaller entrepreneurs, who are very independent and still largely first-generation. Indeed, outside Japan, many companies in other countries in East Asia are just now going through the transition to second-generation entrepreneurship. Singapore is somewhat different in that the entrepreneurial class there is really quite weak. The Singapore strategy has been, therefore, to get multinational corporations involved. Accordingly these corporations have an influence that takes the place of the entrepreneurial class. This was their strategy and it has been successful. So, a comparison of these places reveals striking differences. The question then, is, what is the common pattern? One is their receptivity to the state and the state's concern with economic growth. A second is the long time horizons used for economic planning. Hong Kong may be an exception, probably because of the 1997 deadline, but on the whole, Vogel feels that, as a generalization, most East Asian countries have a longer time horizon than, say, the current U.S. one.

Tu, picking up on Vogel's mention of the role of the state, said that he had the feeling that in East Asia the state was more powerful than the civic society, even in Hong Kong, which is often cited as an example of free enterprise. But now the strength of the Hong Kong government is clearly seen in a number of areas. Tu pointed out that the conceptual resources we have for analysis between politics and economics are somewhat inadequate in trying to understand the dynamics of East Asian societies, for example, initiatives of the market, on the one hand, and state direction, on the other, private versus public, civil society versus a command economy directed by the state, and so on. Government economic leadership needs to be distinguished from the sort of command economy practiced in the PRC. What is the role of the government? What kind of leadership does it provide?

Vogel responded that the answer to these questions differs in each of the countries. In Taiwan, government has been somewhat more reserved than in Korea and Japan in giving clear direction to the economy. They have concentrated more on financial controls. Also, they have had state-sponsored upstream industries, with a strategy of producing products such as petrochemicals, steel, and electric power that downstream producers could use at a low cost. After the oil shock, they made sure to keep the prices low so that the entrepreneurs could keep the prices of their own products competitive.

In Korea, Pak Chung-hee took a much more interventionist role and built up big corporations as fast as he could, on Japan's model, and pushed them to move quickly, thereby assuming great debts and taking considerable risks.

In Singapore, the situation was, said Vogel, quite different, because Lee Kwan Yew had no respect for local entrepreneurs. He felt that they were incompetent and snubbed them, embarrassed them, and looked down on them in public. He felt rather that multinational corporations had the modern entrepreneurial skills Singapore needed.

In Hong Kong, the British rulers tended to be restrained, but in the 1950s and 1960s they began to take more responsibility for the economy and worked well in supporting local entrepreneurs, especially after the fire in 1954, and gradually developed a vision of how to manage things. In the meantime, many of the *shanghui*, the merchant associations, played a greater role than their counterparts elsewhere.

Chang Hao commented that the range of policies and outlook Vogel had just spoken of was just what was found in the Confucian *jingshi* tradition. Almost from the outset of the tradition there were two contrasting conceptions of the center. One is the heavy center (or rigid center) reflected most clearly in the *Zhouli (The rites of Zhou)*, which was used by many Confucian reformers, especially in early imperial period, for example, from Wang Mang in Han all the way to Wang Anshi in the Song. But, argued Chang, by late imperial China, the concept of the light, more flexible center prevailed. The government was still important, but was willing to leave much initiative to the civil society. However, the government reserved the right to intervene whenever necessary. So, these these two predominant conceptions of the center existed. The light, flexible center is reflected in statecraft compilations from Yuan to Ming to Qing. In these formulations the government is active, but also restrained and flexible and willing to leave much initiative to civil society.

Joanna Handlin Smith followed up on Chang's comments, noting that when the *jingshi* gained much importance in the late sixteenth century, there were signs that Confucianism, that is, the body of beliefs practiced by those in official or gentry positions, was undergoing changes that showed the shaping, to some extent, by economic change. For example, emphasis on, and condemnation of, desires that motivate seeking of profit. The morality books that became popular during this period, even among officials and scholars of high note, involved a kind of accounting scheme with merits and demerits being tallied at the end of each month or ten days. This definitely reflects, Handlin Smith feels, a merchant mentality, even in the practical behavior: policies of reducing taxes on merchants, the engagement of brokers and financial managers in local institutions of social welfare, and an appreciation of how investments can be made for the well-being of the community and that in order to do this, one must also gratify the desires and interests of the merchants. Also, there are even examples of scholars, presumably practicing Confucian scholars, unabashedly enjoying their wealth and even spending it on a lavish scale, which serves their goals of becoming centers of social networks. Much of this is mitigated, Handlin Smith continued, by Confucian values: a concern for balance, a concern for order, a concern for some sort of equity, so that expenditure on the self is balanced by some sort of contribution to the community at large. Much more research needs to be done on this period and the whole *jingshi* tradition that was developing out of it. Stacking up against the thirty volumes of the *Kogyo iken* are the thirty volumes of the *Huang ming jingshi wenbian* and many other outpourings, albeit maybe not on quite a coherent scale, that should be examined more to develop an understanding of how ideas were changing.

Rosovsky asked when these works were written.

Handlin Smith replied that they were written in the early seventeenth century and continued in compilations in the early nineteenth century. There are a number of works on economic theory from this period that have not been translated and worked on yet. The question still unanswered is how far this economic development could go. What were the limits on it? But certainly there was a great deal more flexibility in the Confucian economic tradition than has often been thought.

Michael Kalton said that he sensed in the discussion two sides of traditional Confucian discourse that once were unified and maybe are highly problematic in the modern period. In his view, the *jingshi* tradition had much continuity with Confucian political high-tone ethical discourse and in many ways was subordinated to it. In the contemporary period we are looking at how those values were able to be put in a pragmatic framework dealing with the modern economy. The other part of the Confucian discourse has not become pragmatic, and at least in places like South Korea, you have government public political discourse involving moral confrontation. This area, Kalton feels, needs discussion. What room is there for compromise? Can you remain Confucian and become pragmatic? Can you be a moralist and really end up with a workable multiparty system? These are huge questions that might be examined.

Thomas Gold, speaking to the case of Taiwan, said that Taiwan was a good example of what he had been speaking of the previous evening: how do you weigh culture and tradition versus the exigencies of the particular circumstances in defining the type of role the state plays in the economy, the way entrepreneurs behave, and so on. We cannot just look at the Guomindang on Taiwan after 1949. We also must look at the record of the Guomindang on the mainland, where it had a reputation as one of the most venal, brutal, corrupt, and incompetent regimes that had ever existed. The state leaders treated the private economy as their own private playground, and they treated the private sector as something they could manipulate and plunder as they pleased. It was only after they came to Taiwan, with the lesson of having lost the mainland, that there was a deep review of what had happened and they began to change their attitude and redefine the Three Principles of the People and what their role in the economy should be. The Guomindang also in the 1940s and 1950s took a very strong and transformative attitude towards Taiwan society, carrying out a land reform, having huge state enterprises, and so forth. It was only through a certain amount of foreign pressure, Gold argues, that they began to support the idea of a strong private commercial and industrial class. They picked their friends (and selected specific sectors, as well) to become the first generation of entrepreneurs in Taiwan. They created a bifurcated system where politics was the monopoly of the mainlanders, and in the economic sphere Taiwanese were given great, but not total, latitude, because, as Vogel mentioned, the state dominated finance and the upstream industry, and also they controlled much of the agricultural surplus, access to imported goods, and access to export licenses. Some of the most favored businessmen were mainlanders. The state's role has been a dynamic one, shifting over time. It has now retrenched a great deal from its control over the economy, and there has been a process of the emergence of civil society. But there still is much informal activity by the state by means of which they are able to channel or guide much of the economic decision making. One thing, in particular, is the behind-the-scenes pressure to donate to a variety of public causes. We have heard about the Confucian ideal of sharing wealth to aid the community. How much of this is decided by the business person and how much is forced out of him? There has, Gold feels, been a great deal of hagiography written about Taiwan businessmen, often disguising a fairly nefarious past. On the mainland, there is now the sense that the bureaucracy is running the economy as its own private economy. He then asked how the idea of businessmen helping the community was translated into behavior. In practice, is it that the businessmen have internalized the ideal to the extent that they do it on their own, or is it that the government is pressuring them to build schools, establish foundations, and so on?

Rosovsky noted that there was another possibility. It could be argued that in East Asia, unless there is a crisis, there is an assumption that the government acts in the interests of people in general; therefore, it is not really as contested as it would be in, say, American society. Thus, the government is much more powerful vis-à-vis the business sector. It does not have to be coercive, since there is a basic assumption that the bureaucrat acts in the interests of the nation.

Gold agreed, saying that this also tied in with his presentation of the previous evening: that there was an ingrained authoritarian streak and an acceptance of the legitimacy of the government telling you what to do. In Taiwan, Gold believes, one reason many companies are small is that they are worried about attracting too much government attention.

George De Vos asked what the Confucian attitude has been toward population control. There were some documents from the Tokugawa period expressing worry because the farmers were practicing *mabiki*, literally, "thinning," and cutting down the number of children, while the government wanted more children. Was there self-consciousness toward overpopulation in late imperial China? What was the general attitude toward overpopulation?

Tu gave a brief response noting that there was a deep-rooted tradition in China that people were wealth. There was population growth in Japan from Tokugawa times, according to Bill LaFleur, who did demographic studies and was concerned with the role of the government in encouraging population growth. It was very difficult both for the Guomindang and the CCP to develop a comprehensive population control program. Zhou Enlai, as late as 1957, at the suggestion of a demographics expert at Peking University, proposed a population control program to Mao. But Mao rejected it vehemently as a foreign conspiracy against the interests of the Chinese people. In Taiwan, a rigid application of Sun Yat-sen's Three Principles of the People blocked for a long time any population planning.

Rosovsky pointed out that there is a very revisionist school of Japanese demographers that argues that from the middle of the Tokugawa period to the restoration the total population seems to have been stable. There may be argument over this, but some scholars have asserted that the peasants limited the size of their families not because of dire poverty, but because they wished to raise their standard of living. How does this sit with Confucianism?

Tu said this is not Confucian at all. This is totally different from the situation found in China. Although there was infanticide there, often of female children, it was almost always done in dire circumstances such as famine.

Rozman noted that in Tokugawa Japan the communities got together and tried to limit the number of households. There was a perception that carried over into the late Meiji period at least that Japan was in danger of squandering its resources with population. He does not see this as an issue of Confucian or non-Confucian. Confucian values, he believes, stressed trying to maximize long-term family resources and planning for the future of the family. It so happened that the Chinese interpreted this very differently from the Japanese.

Schwartz said that they had not talked of the goal of all of this for a while: wealth and power. This is a very ambiguous goal, no matter what the means used. Maybe the same economic philosophy prevailed under the Guomindang on the mainland, but the situations were highly different. So he would agree that the external situation in which one finds oneself is very important. But even in the case of Japan, when Schwartz taught modern Japanese history right after World War II, the major issue was how Japanese development had led to this enormous disaster. Why had Japan gone astray by developing so much! Coming out of the New Deal, Schwartz feels that it is quite appropriate for the government to play a role in the economy, albeit not as a centrally planned economy. There are other areas of life where he would not feel such a role is justifiable. Furthermore, he is not sure that all private power is civic society. There can also, he would argue, be sinister growth of organized wealth.

Rosovsky asked Eckert to sum up.

Eckert said that at least one idea had emerged in the session: The role of government in East Asia, whether we want to call it Confucian or not, seems to be more pronounced and more acceptable in an East Asian context than we are accustomed to thinking of it in the West. He would add to this that there are still limits to this role, although they may be much narrower than those in, say, the United States, still they exist. This brings up the subject of coercion. There are, for example, definitely Korean businessmen who felt coerced by the Chon Tu-hwan regime and have said so publicly. Also, in line with Vogel's observations, it could well be that the limits are different in the different countries. Korea traditionally had a very strong civil society with a very strong aristocratic class that penetrated society and was likely quite different, Eckert feels, from China or Japan. There may be, for that reason, less tolerance for intervention in the Korean case than in other societies in East Asia.

Rosovsky had a suggestion for pursuing this topic further: Everyone should take major strategic variables in economic development and examine them specifically from the point of view of, say, Confucian ideology and practice, capital accumulation and savings, attitudes toward technological change, labor discipline, and so forth, and study it in some detail at that level. By so doing, it should be possible, Rosovsky feels, to build a model (he avers that he hesitates to use this term in front of Schwartz) that might provide a basis for further discussion.

Popular Thought and Religion

HENRY ROSOVSKY CALLED on Tu Weiming to introduce the topic.

Tu pointed out that the workshop had been organized, more or less, in a series of concentric circles, very much in keeping with the vision of the *Great Learning*. Starting with the question of the self, it then has moved on to issues of the family, the community, the state and political economy, and then beyond. The outer realm should never be closed: there always is the possibility of going beyond. Therefore the highest ideal in the Confucian tradition is not a form of anthropocentrism, but rather the unity of humanity and heaven. More seriously, one question that needs to be confronted is whether Confucianism is a religion or not. It may have been functioning as a substitute for a certain kind of religious order in traditional Chinese society. But according to, say, Wilfred Cantwell Smith, it is not a religion in that particular sense. So, what is Confucian spirituality? Another aspect of the tradition that has already been touched upon is the question of whether Confucianism is a form of elite culture in such a way that it is diametrically opposed to popular religious ideas? Or, has Confucianism been so much an integral part of popular consciousness that we can actually identify, if not vulgarized, at least popularized Confucian ideas in syncretic religions of various kinds? Scholars involved in anthropological research of various kinds will be able to share their insights with us.

James Watson began by addressing the whole issue of "Confucianism," which he always puts in quotation marks because he felt he was having difficulty identifying what it is and what it is not. Benjamin Schwartz had earlier raised the interesting question of what if this had been a workshop on Christian culture and its modern transformations (at the risk of putting words in his mouth). What, in other words, is "Christian" about Thatcher's Britain or Papandreou's Greece? Returning to China, what is Confucian about Chinese peasant popular culture, or what Roderick MacFarquhar referred to earlier as "vulgarized Confucianism"? The short answer is, if you listen to anthropologists who have done field work in Taiwan, Hong Kong, and the PRC, precious little. Anthropologists who work on the ground in Chinese cultural areas tend to be very suspicious of the "Confucian" label. It tends to be a catchall phrase, a kind of box that will hold almost anything. Therefore, the usual anthropological wisdom has it that this label is essentially meaningless, and anthropologists spend considerable time debunking the whole idea. In other words, if it can mean everything, then it means nothing. So, we need to disentangle or dissect the label of "Confucian." Watson warned the group that he was speaking from a somewhat narrow perspective on Chinese society. His image of it comes from living and working in Cantonese villages: in Hong Kong, in the New Territories, and more recently, in the Pearl River delta. Further, he disclaimed any great knowledge about high culture and philosophical debates, but argued that this was also the case in the people he lived with.

His major focus for the presentation was on one central aspect often labeled "Confucian," namely, the issue of clan and lineage organization, extradomestic kinship organization, and by implication the Chinese ancestor-worship cult. This package of cultural traits is often labeled "Confucian." The values expressed therefore are thought to be a reflection of some sort of grand Confucian tradition that has been passed down from the Han dynasty to the present. But in what sense is it "Confucian"? If you view lineage organizations from within, from the ground up, the activities and the values expressed hardly measure up to the high-minded ethical standard that one finds in the *Analects*, Zhu Xi, and elsewhere. Lineages, in other words, are not (as some would have it from the literature) welfare institutions, as the rhetoric of scholar-bureaucrats would have it.

Lineages, looked at internally as they operate every day, are hard-nosed business corporations run by steely eyed managers who guard corporate property jealously. In other words, far from any notion of generalized reciprocity or generalized idea of welfare. Lineages are based on corporate property, usually land, and the problem in Chinese lineages has always been to keep people out—not, in other words, to bring more people in and to be magnanimous and to spread the wealth—and to draw a boundary delineating clearly who is a member and who is not.

This is quite contrary to the rhetoric that is represented to the outside world about Chinese kinship groups. If you listen to what people say about kinship groups, you get the "Confucian" image of what is being done. If you pay attention to the actions and what is done every day, you find that it is quite the opposite. Hence, there is a preoccupation with patrilineal descent. In other words, demonstrated, known descent from key ancestors is essential for defining who is and who is not a member of the corporation.

From one perspective, the interest in descent and lines of kinship may embrace a kind of Confucian filial-piety image, but from a hard-nosed business corporation perspective, it has the opposite effect: defining who is and who is not a member of that group. So the ethos within a lineage is always drawn between us and them. There are those of us who are members and who have rights to this land and this corporation and everyone else outside is "them." It is a very closed ideology that operates internally.

The Chinese ancestor-worship cult is part of this closed ideological system and, Watson argues, is not based on notions of benign filial piety. Quite the opposite. Reverence and respect for ancestors and, by implication, living elders has a very practical concern. Rather than a system as it might be represented in the Confucian notions of kinship, ancestor worship is a form of generalized reciprocity; it is a form of exchange between the living and the dead.

Interestingly enough, the balance of power in the Chinese ancestral cult tends to shift from the dead to the living as the dead increase in age. In other words, among those Watson studied, there was the notion that after dying a biological death it was possible to continue to exist in the afterlife. As you age as an ancestor, you become more and more dependent on the living. Wealthy and powerful lineages build elaborate ancestor halls with ancestral tablets and have elaborate rituals at the ancestral tombs. The fascinating thing about this in south China is that every dime that is paid for the ancestral rites and for the upkeep of the ancestral halls comes from the dead themselves, from their estates. It is managed by a living manager. So when the money from an estate runs out, the ancestors are forgotten, and therefore, essentially, they die a second death. Inevitably all ancestors are destined for a second death in the afterlife. The dead, in other words, must be deemed to have produced benefits in order to survive. The benefits for the living have to be wealth, power, or progeny in order to keep that exchange going. Once the ancestors stop producing, they are terminated.

There are many examples in south China of weak kinship groups who have essentially killed their own ancestors. In Cantonese, they say that their ancestors are *moyong* (Mandarin *meiyu yong*—"useless"). They take the tablets out of the ancestral hall, soak them in kerosene, and set fire to them and kill off their ancestors, essentially saying, "To hell with you! You're not producing, so we're not going to venerate you anymore. We're going to start over again with a new set of ancestors." They do this without renewal and without rewriting tablets. The idea is that there can be no such thing as a freeloading ancestor, basking in the glow of some sort of generalized filial piety. Ancestors have really got to produce! So, in other words, the realm of ancestor worship for those who participate internally is a very tough social Darwinist environment. It is not the notion of generalized filial piety operating.

Now, this being the case, what does it say about Confucianism and its influence on the popular culture? Anthropologists have, as mentioned previously, a kind of extreme form of cynicism; they tend to be very cynical about these types of institutions. Perhaps because we spend too much time living in these communities and seeing all the activities involved, we often find it difficult to sit back and generalize about the wider culture. Anthropologists as cynics also accuse intellectual historians of fixating on the self-serving rhetoric of scholar-bureaucrats who write about all these institutions. In other words, just as Gold described the hagiographic treatment of Taiwan businessmen, many anthropologists would argue that something similar is going on when the scholar-bureaucrats represent the popular cultural view of ancestor worship and kinship organizations. Watson said that he feels this is, in a sense, an unfair characterization on the part of anthropologists of what intellectual historians actually do. What he had represented was a view of ancestor cult and lineage organizations from within, with everyday operations. From an external perspective, things appear to be very different, once you look at the rhetoric of what people are describing. There has been recent work on what anthropologists and historians have been calling "lineage building" or the creation of kinship groups in the T'ang-Song transition, the Song, and later in the Ming that is quite relevant here. The question is: who actually creates these kinship groups, and for what purpose? How do they evolve? Is it a consequence of active creation by leading bureaucrats, as, for instance, if you follow the research by Dennis Twitchett on the Fan charitable estates? He discusses the representations of men such as Fan Zhongyan as being lineage builders for, if you read the rhetoric, benevolent purposes. In other words, can one argue that these kinship groups are constructed from the top down, Confucian-inspired efforts of social engineering by bureaucrats and scholars as reflected in the high-minded rhetoric of the records?

Watson confessed that, until recently, anthropologists such as himself who had done research in rural localities saw lineage building as a clear consequence of local political and economic conditions and argued that scholar-bureaucrats had very little to do with kinship groups and that they were merely the followers and not the leaders of these cultural developments. That, in other words, the scholar-bureaucrats could only ride the tiger of local culture and try to steer it in the direction they wanted it to go, and if they did not succeed in that, then they could write their high-minded rhetorical records about what happened. Later, historians are left with the cultural debris of that era, which of course is the written record of the cultural elite who were writing it from their perspectives. This is a standard anthropological attack on intellectual history.

More recently, anthropologists, including Watson, have begun to work more closely with historians. Accordingly, the views of both historians and anthropologists have begun to change. For the past decade, Watson has worked with historians such as Patricia Ebrey at the University of Illinois, David Johnson at U.C. Berkeley, Evelyn Rawski at Pittsburgh, Susan Naquin at the University of Pennsylvania, and a number of other social and intellectual historians who are interested in such things as kinship. This recent research shows some very interesting processes involved in lineage building and the creation of ritual systems. It begins to look as if the process was a two-way feedback process involving, on the one hand, the co-optation of popular developments by scholar-bureaucrats and the emulation of elite models by local people, on the other hand. Both processes are working. An example is the ancestral hall, which many anthropologists would have argued years ago had little to do with elite culture. In fact, if you go back to the records, you can find that the actual physical architectural representation of the hall is borrowed directly from the representations of the scholar-bureaucratic models of the Song period. Fan Zhongyan and others were involved in this. Another example is that of funeral rites. These essentially were local developments that were accepted and reinterpreted, both from the classics and from local practice molded by higher elites and essentially reentered into a textual tradition. In other words, it was a feedback process, both up and down.

The interesting aspect of this up-and-down and down-and-up process in cultural construction is that when one looks at China from an anthropological perspective, unlike some other societies, the Chinese tend to agree to agree that creations represent acceptable Confucian form. In other words, it is the agreement to agree that is so fascinating. You can call it whatever you want. You can call it a Confucian construction and it could be accepted as such because you essentially are creating the impression of a centralized culture by following the high-text models. It really does not matter, Watson argues, what people do with those models as long as they follow the form. In the interest of all people, you can follow these forms and interpret them accordingly. So it serves local interests and it serves the interests of the state and local elites as well. So all parties say, when you ask them about kinship groups and ancestor-worship patterns or rituals of all kinds, something like the following: "Oh, yes, this is following the tenets of Confucius. This is an expression of filial piety, *xiao*." They can all say that, and they all believe it and agree to agree. The process, then, of ideological convergence, agreeing to agree, is, Watson would argue, essentially the glue that helps hold Sinitic societies together: Japan, China, and Korea. In other words, it is the creation of the illusion of unity and interpretive agreement that is a fascinating process.

George De Vos earlier was speaking of ritual, and Tu asked Watson to say

something about it. Watson said that he had written a paper that argued that
the key to the construction of Chineseness is the acceptance of ritual form,
very much as De Vos and Wang Gungwu were saying. From Watson's perspective, it is the acceptance of the form and the agreement of what the form means
that sets Sinitic societies apart from others. Rather than orthodoxy or correct
belief, it is orthopraxy or correct practice that matters. If one behaves properly
and acts properly, then one can become Chinese or Confucian or whatever
label you want to affix to it. The emphasis is on external form. A good example
is that of rites of passage. To become Chinese or maintain Chineseness there
are key rites of passage that need to be performed according to Chinese forms.
One is marriage and the other is funerals. There are certain things that must
be done in these rituals. There is a sequence of nine ritual acts that have to be
performed at a funeral. If those nine essential acts are performed, then it is a
Chinese funeral. And then it is possible to do whatever one wants to with the
corpse: it can be buried, burned, hanged in trees, or whatever. The Chinese
did all of those. But it was the performance of the funeral act that essentially
made it a Chinese performance. Also, you could believe anything you wanted
to about the efficacy of those acts; that was not the issue—the issue was the
performance. Watson would argue that there was never a set of ideological
constructs that made one Chinese. One did not convert to a creed to become
Chinese. This was very different from the European tradition. In Christianity,
the main debate was the Eucharist. It was not so much how the Eucharist was
performed as what it meant. Watson argues that it is impossible to find a similar
set of dialogues about the meaning of ritual in Sinitic cultures. It is the
performance of the rites that matters, not the meaning of those rites. Watson
looks at kinship groups and ancestor worship from a similar perspective. It is
not what people carry in their heads that matters; it is what they did on the
ground that made them Confucian or Chinese or whatever.

Kim Kwang-ok spoke on the influence of Confucianism upon popular
consciousness in South Korea. It is important to put Confucianism in the
context of social class when discussing Confucian culture as a social-political-
ethical system. Also we need to understand Confucian culture as it is practiced
in the everyday life of ordinary people in a contemporary social environment.

In Korea the Confucian tradition is strong enough to be institutionalized.
As far as he knows, only in Korea is Confucianism still practiced through
organizations. Also there can be seen the process of reinvention of tradition,
which is also the socio-cultural manifestation of the formation of new political
groupings. It is the result of estate grouping disorganizing or disengaging, but
of increasing integration. It is not only the outcome of conservatism, but also

that of dynamic socio-cultural change that is brought about by a new alignment of power. This means that they are now faced with a new situation where struggle and competition for power resources and privilege between groups is inevitable, for example, the competition between Christian groups and Buddhist groups. As a consequence, within the framework of a formal political system, they manipulate customs, myths, symbols, values, and ceremonies from their own cultural tradition in order to articulate an informal political organization that is used as a weapon in the struggle.

In Korea it can be seen that the institutional Confucians maintain and expand their network at the national as well as local level. Their headquarters are the Songgyun'gwan (the National Academy during the Choson dynasty) in Seoul, and in the countryside are the *hyanggyo* (former sites of government schools in the Choson period, now used as meeting halls and schools for the Confucian organization) and *sowon* (private academies). There are many rituals and ceremonies still observed where high-ranking local officials are invited. Continuously they have developed and refined their own language, dress, decorum, and even their hobbies. Also, they acquire specialized genealogical knowledge and hold philosophical discussions. This organization of Confucian elites is called the Yulim (lit. "forest of Confucians"). Its members claim that a proper eliteness cannot be learned from books alone, but that only a man of noble origins (i.e., *yangban* class) can cultivate himself enough to gain elite qualities through continuous participation in the socialization process open exclusively to the *yangban* class. These impart such things as gestures, accent, and special speech behavior, politeness, self-respect, pride, decency, and delicacy of thought, taste and propriety, generosity, loyalty toward tradition, and a firm attitude toward any challenge from the outside. These qualities are all part of the distinct repertoire of eliteness.

Kim asked why this sort of culture has developed more and more, despite modernization. One important approach involves political dynamics. For example, it was encouraged by President Pak Chung-hee, who at first criticized the Confucian tradition since it was quite opposite his goal of modernization. He ridiculed and criticized many Confucian leaders in history. Then he learned about the power of the Confucian elites during his presidential campaign when he praised Yi Yulgok highly because he had foreseen the problem of national security in the sixteenth century and had urged preparation against a possible invasion by the Japanese. At the same time, he criticized Kim Song-il as the most vivid example of the traditional elite intoxicated by loyalty only to their own family and personal cliques at the expense of the national interest because he denied the possibility of a Japanese invasion in the 1590s. This public criticism of Kim Song-il was met by severe protest from the Confucian elites, especially those of the Yongnam area, since Kim was one of the famed historical representatives of that region.

Among the Confucians there are two broad schools. One is the Yongnam (southeast) school; the other is the Kiho (central) school. The former region—from which the last three presidents, Pak Chung-hee, Chon Tu-hwan, and Roh Tae-woo, came—is represented philosophically by Yi T'oegye. The Kiho school, on the other hand, is linked philosophically to Yi Yulgok.

Realizing that the Yongnam area was his political stronghold, Pak Chung-hee tried to consolidate his political power base by gaining the support of Confucians from that area. He renovated Tosan Academy, the school associated with Yi T'oegye, and Yi was honored as the greatest scholar in national history. Also, portraits of Yi T'oegye and Yi Yulgok were put on the currency. So not only at the local level, but also at the national level, the conflict and compromise between these two factions are still in evidence. Without an understanding of their interaction, an understanding of the dynamics of politics in contemporary South Korea is impossible.

Koreans are very much concerned with nationalism in the face of foreign elements: political, economic, and cultural. This trend is particularly strong among college students. For them, the Confucian tradition is a symbol of national identity and cultural purity. So it is becoming more popular among younger people. But still, the most important point is that the Confucian tradition is very active at the local level in politics. In order to be active in local politics, one should be a member of the Yulim group, or at least one should get its support. In order to do this, it is important to have genealogical knowledge, not only about one's own ancestors but also those of other important lineage groups in the community, so that he can clarify his own ancestors' relationships to those of others when he meets them. In Korea, when introducing oneself, information concerning lineage affiliation is often given, including any great figures in one's family line. This also includes knowledge of affinal connections and marriage connections.

Knowledge about ceremony and ritual is also very important in determining one's qualification for membership in the elite group. Ancestor worship, as well as rites of passage, including weddings and funerals, are strictly formalized and should be closely observed. Also, many aspects of behavior in everyday life are ritualized, and one is expected to observe them completely. It is not seldom that people of the elite class argue and criticize each other for different interpretations of ritual process or ceremonial procedures. This is a strong point of contention between members of the Yongnam and Kiho schools. It is not possible to determine whose view is correct, nor is it terribly important to do so. What *is* important for a Confucian elite is having one's own point of view in a discussion of ethics and ritual knowledge.

The elite collaborate informally through the exclusive network of amity, a map of primary relationships that are governed by moral rights and obligations and are objectified and kept alive. An outsider may succeed in acquiring external trappings such as clothing, housing, and other items of conspicuous consumption, but he will not thereby automatically become affiliated within the power elite and partake of its privileges. To do so, he must achieve the much more difficult task of grafting himself onto the inner network of power relationships that links the members of the group together. It is this inner, highly exclusive network that provides the real basis for identity and serves as a system of channels for collaboration and developing and maintaining the interests of its members.

The proliferation of activities and organizational development of Confucian elite groups is not the result of Korean society being unchanged. Rather, it comes out of social changes, which have produced a complicated competition of newly emerged groups for political resources. The exploitation of class culture in the informal articulation of political interests has been observed almost everywhere in the world. What is of special interest to anthropologists and political scientists is the manner and the process by which cultural norms, values, myths, and symbols are made to express a number of organizational functions that are essential for political organization by these groups. Every political group must mobilize its resources in order to find solutions to a number of organizational problems, including problems of distinctiveness, political communication, decision making, authority, ideology, and discipline. Formal political groups organize these functions legally and bureaucratically, while informal groups organize them through the idiom of custom. So Confucians try to emphasize their distinctiveness because they want to maintain their hereditary social network for political opportunity in the midst of drastic social change, on the one hand, and to apply traditional criteria to measure the quality of life, on the other, since they believe the present situation of disintegration of the social system is a result of the people having lost their traditional system.

John Berthrong spoke on the reemergence of a Confucian–Christian dialogue in a formal sense as commissioner to the unit on dialog of the World Council of Churches. This unit is a recent phenomenon. After Vatican II the Roman Catholic Church set up a number of commissions designed to begin dialog with other faith communities. The World Council of Churches followed along and by the early 1970s had a unit on dialog, which then began to choose partners for various multilateral conversations. The first ones were somewhat predictable: with the Jewish communities, with Muslim communities, with Hinduism, with Buddhism, and with the Sikh community. There were three Christian-Buddhist conferences: in 1980, in 1984, and in 1987. Participants in the 1984 conference decided it might be necessary, interesting, and profitable to have a Confucian-Christian dialog. So this formally went through the structure of the World Council of Churches and was set up to take place in Hong Kong in the summer of 1988, cosponsored by the World Council of Churches, the Christian Center for Study of Chinese Culture and Religion, and the Chinese University of Hong Kong.

One very important question for the organizers was: Who is a Confucian? Actually it really turned out to be an easy question at one level, for a living dialog. It was simply decided that a Confucian is a person who says that he or she is a Confucian and is so recognized as such by his or her community. We relied on advice from people such as Tu Weiming, Liu Shuxian (Liu Shu-hsien), and Chen Zhongying (Cheng Chung-ying). The people chosen were those who both described Confucianism as accurately as possible and commended it as having values appropriate to the modern age, not only to East Asian cultures, but also to the emerging global village.

The meeting had about seventy participants, drawn primarily from East Asia. There were delegations from the PRC, Korea, Singapore, Taiwan, and North America, and a few stray Europeans, but no delegation from Japan. The meeting proved successful, so now it will be institutionalized for the life of the subunit on dialog. It was agreed to have more such meetings. The next is scheduled for Berkeley in 1990 and the one following at Beijing University in 1992.

Berthrong next surveyed the kinds of issues that emerged at the conference. The first was a debate on transcendence and immanence that seemed to be of equal interest to the Confucians and the Christians. It used to be fairly clear from a Confucian perspective that Christians are quite interested in transcendence, say theism of various sorts, and from a Christian perspective, the Confucians seem very interested in immanence and not transcendence. People discovered that, at least in the contemporary world, those are much more blurred categories. This topic came up over and over and has been designated as one of the formal discussion pieces for the next session. Many of the Confucians, interestingly enough, felt they needed to discuss with the Christians just what transcendence means in both traditions. The influence of Mou Zongsan (Mou Tsung-san), though he was not in attendance, was very pervasive. He argues in his writings that Confucianism is a religious tradition (though its modes of organization are different from Judaism, Hinduism, Islam, etc.) in that it has practical, everyday-life orientations, and it nurtures the seeds of incipient transcendence. It has, therefore, its own inherent understanding of transcendence. Paraphrased in a Christian way, we might say that one needs to get right with the *tiandao* in order to achieve self-transformation, the learning for the sake of the self and others that is so crucial to Confucian spirituality.

The second topic that came up was the question of "dual citizenship." Can a Confucian be a Christian and can a Christian be a Confucian? Many of the Confucians were quite willing to pursue the following train of thought. They argued that the classical Confucian and neo-Confucian tradition is really rather neutral about the claims of theism: it was not a *problematique*. So, the argument went, could a modern Confucian be a theist without violating any of the deep grammar of the Confucian tradition? Some of the people there felt that, yes, it might be possible to graft onto Confucianism, as a living tradition, notions of theism and be perfectly Confucian. Some of them even went farther and said that they would consider themselves to be Christian Confucians.

There was a good deal of discussion about taking a careful look again at some of the writings of the Ming Christians, people like Yang Tingyun, and the kind of thought that they propounded, much to the consternation of their fellow Confucians, the Buddhists, and the Jesuits. Yang argued very strongly that he was a Confucian. He was very much part of the national elite and saw theism as answering a number of personal conundrums. But that simply helped him as a Confucian.

Berthrong pointed out that this was not an argument that had a great deal of initial appeal in ecumenical Christian circles. But this kind of discussion of dual citizenship is very difficult, even in World Council circles. "Contextualization" is in favor, but dual citizenship smacks of the dread religious disease of syncretism. Yet the challenge was made.

It was also asked whether, if there could be Christian Confucians, could there also be Confucian Christians? And what would that mean for Christian theology. Again it was left hanging in those early discussions. This whole topic will be raised in World Council circles and will likely be an ongoing part of these conversations over the next few years. These discussions are likely to have an impact on East Asian Christian self-identity, and are fascinating for Confucian self-identity as well.

De Vos asked whether Confucianism can exist by itself, or must it always coexist with some other religious practices that round it out? Can you have Confucianism without Taoism or some other kind of religious practices that satisfy some individuals who are in a Confucian culture? It struck De Vos that the World Council of Churches has a very ethnocentric notion of logic, that one must be logically consistent in religious issues. In Korea the system was worked out quite nicely, with shamanic and Confucian practices coexisting, so that when a man does his ancestor worship with a benign concept, perhaps, of ancestry, women take care of the other malevolent possibilities through other practices that ward off the baleful influences of the dead.

Tu said that from a comparative religious perspective it was fascinating to attempt to locate the Confucian tradition. On the one hand, there are world religions—Christianity, Islam, and Buddhism—in the sense that there is no particular cultural form that is distinctive. There are also culturally specific religious traditions, such as Shintoism. Confucianism is somewhere in between. It is neither as specific to Chinese culture as Shintoism is to Japanese culture, nor is it so universalizable that it can go beyond the East Asian cultural context. The other point is that Confucianism, like Hinduism, is not a membership religion. It is in this sense that the whole question about religious identity arises. Reischauer has pointed out that in Japan maybe 70 percent of the people identify themselves as Shintoist and 80 percent as Buddhists. If you ask them if they are neo-Confucians, they will not know what you are talking about. Yet if you are not sensitive to some of the issues raised here at the workshop, then a very important dimension of dimension, as well as practice will be missed.

Rosovsky asked Tu why Confucianism was ever called a religion.

Tu responded that this was a very new phenomenon occurring in the West after the seventeenth century (as discussed in a recent book published by Wilfred Cantwell Smith called *The Meaning and End of Religion*). They began to talk of other religious traditions such as Hinduism, Mohammedism, Confucianism, Taoism, Judaism, and so on, as opposed to Christianity. This was very much a new creation, a reification of a way of life and spiritual orientation because of the post-Enlightenment need for some sort of consensual understanding of the faiths of other people. The question of whether Confucianism is a religion or not has never been raised within the Chinese cultural context. And it has never been answered by scholars who have raised it in a Western fashion. It is still highly debatable. However, if you do not look at Confucianism as an organized religion—the question of whether there are religious dimensions and forms of religiosity and spirituality in the Confucian tradition—if you do not address that issue and simply talk about it as an ethical system, you miss much, because you do not understand how it functioned traditionally or in the modern context.

The revival of Confucianism is an intriguing phenomenon; it is the emergence of self-conscious identification. It has never happened before, since there was no need before the May Fourth period to term oneself a Confucian, because before this everyone would just have assumed that you were one. In the post–May Fourth period, due to the iconoclastic attack on Confucianism, the conditions have drastically changed. Now in southeast Asia, Taiwan, Hong Kong, and a number of other places, we see the emergence of a communal, critical self-awareness of some of the Confucian intellectuals identifying themselves very clearly. It is a self-construction. This leads, Tu feels, to all sorts of interesting ethical-religious implications, which may or may not turn out to be practical.

The situation in mainland China is particularly intriguing. A recent bibliography of studies on Confucianism (and not the Confucian tradition) for the last five years contained more than one thousand items (articles and books) with about five hundred authors. Right now the largest research project under the sponsorship of the Educational Commission in the area of the history of philosophy is what they call "new Confucianism." This is a term that has been applied to Tu himself, and he noted that he had never known that he was a new Confucian. But once this term is applied, it can never be gotten away from. For this research there are, all together, thirty volumes planned, under the leadership of Fang Keli. They identified ten new Confucians from two generations: the May Fourth generation and the post–World War II generation. The first generation includes five members (Liang Shuming, Zhang Junmai, Feng Youlan, He Lin [Ho Lin], Xiong Shili), as does the second generation (Mou Zongsan, Tang Junyi, Xu Fuguan, Qian Mu, Fang Dongmei). It is very interesting that separate consultations in Taiwan and Singapore independently came up with almost the exactly the same list.

Peter Bol, as one who "describes rather than commends" the *ru* tradition, noted the exclusivistic, elitist dimension to the *ru* undertaking, as well documented in Kim's presentation. Could we, he asked, imagine a peasant in one of Watson's villages calling himself a *rujia*? And be recognized by his community as such? Or is not that community in fact necessarily an elite scholarly community that gives that recognition?

Chang Hao said that, in fact, this had happened in the past, in the Wang Yangming school, in the late Ming period.

Bol continued by arguing that once the issue becomes people as individuals claiming to be *ru* and having communities to recognize that (noting that he was not equating the term *shi* with *ru*), then this term and this concept as an intellectual and moral role has been redefined through history. He suspects that if we examined the list of those who attended the World Council of Churches meeting, we would find that, by and large, they were Song–Ming neo-Confucians, or those who were inspired by the Song–Ming intellectual tradition, the *daoxue* tradition and the *xinxue* tradition, and not, for example, the later *kaozheng* (evidential) tradition. And yet, from the perspective of intellectual history, the evidential research movement of the eighteenth century is part of the Confucian tradition. But are these people *ru*, or have they in fact become something else, scholars? Is Yu Yingshi a Confucian, for example? Or is he a historian? While noting that this does not preclude the possibility of what it means to be a *ru* getting redefined, Bol said that he is struck by the need of those who want to call themselves Confucians to find justification of their definitions, in their own tradition.

Schwartz addressed himself to issues that Watson had raised. He said he wished to press how cynical Watson really was. On the topic of the family as an interest unit, when one speaks of an individual as the "economic man" it is quite clear. But as soon as one moves beyond this to a group, and says, "We as a group have common interests," the question of what kind of group it is that says this becomes important. Anthropologists often assert that in all cultures it is the lineage that is the interest group. For example, in Greek culture there are often clusters of war bands that are a self-interested group. Surely, he asked, Watson was not saying that ancestor worship was invented, as it were, consciously for the purpose of serving the interests of those practicing it. Or, maybe the causation goes two ways. The fact that there is an orientation towards ancestor worship may also have some influence on the fact that one makes this the interest group. In American society, we do not form interest alliances with our second cousins; we usually do not think you have the slightest thing in common with them. So why this should become *the* interest group is interesting, particularly because in later Chinese history it is often quite self-conscious. Sometimes families fall apart and are only reestablished by a conscious decision. Schwartz would agree that high Confucian culture does arise out of ancestor worship. But the whole question is that, yes, in many religious phenomena one expects a kind of contract relation with the gods. So he finds many issues here. Maybe, he speculated, the orientation toward ancestor worship has something to do with the family becoming the focus of interest grouping.

Second, about ritual orthopraxy, there have been, Schwartz said, large groups of Han Chinese who have not engaged in orthopraxy (from a Confucian point of view) and have, for example, gone into Buddhist monasteries. Then there were those, such as the Seven Sages of the Bamboo Grove, who rejected the whole thing out of hand. He finds it a shaky way of defining the Chinese as Chinese. Furthermore, there have been debates down through the ages about rituals. Now maybe this has been an activity of the high culture. But there have been long debates about proper literature. Now this *jingshi* literature is often called "statecraft," involving what Westerners observed as water control and money systems. But there also are huge portions of this work that are concerned with the question of what are the right rituals. All kinds of fierce debates.

Watson agreed but added: it's the form.

Schwartz continued, saying there is a notion that the real rituals of the past have been completely forgotten. New rituals have been developed later on in time. As a monodefinition of Han he finds it rather shaky. Of course, Schwartz noted, some Chinese define themselves as Han, even though they totally rejected the entire ritual system. He feels that he is fairly cynical in dealing with the relationship between ideals and realities in all cultures, including Western academic culture. But what is a we-group, an interest group?

Watson responded that part of the problem is that in presenting a capsule summary of his arguments he tends to be far more polemic than in writing. He would never argue that any society is necessarily organized by orthopractic or orthodox means. In almost every society there is a blend, a mix. The argument that he would make is that, granting a continuum of cultures, taking European Christian societies at certain times, there is far more preoccupation with creed and belief, that there is much more concern about what happens in people's heads in certain European societies at certain times, for example, the Inquisition and the idea that the Eucharist is not just a matter of how you perform it, but what you believe about it. In Chinese societies, he would argue, it mattered less what people believed about actions as long as one performed properly. But, of course, this does not mean that there was not a uniform belief system underpinning it. He would simply argue that in a Sinic context it is much more important to perform properly than to carry a correct set of beliefs.

Concerning the other point about lineage and cynicism, he said that this is probably changing among most anthropologists. The cynicism develops primarily among anthropologists who work in lineage-type communities and have very little perspective on larger Chinese issues. In the last ten years Watson feels that his work with historians has broadened his perspective and that he is beginning to see that, in fact, the representation he had developed of kinship groups earlier is definitely a skewed vision.

Ancestor worship is an interesting issue. K. C. Chang says that we can find ancestor worship in China as far back as there are written records. Watson's response to this is that ancestor worship means different things in different periods in history. The idea that ancestor worship today, and in the late imperial period, could have been different from what it was in the Han and the Song is quite obvious. What Watson wanted to point out is that, from one perspective, it is a misconception of ancestor worship to see it as a reflection of filial piety. From another perspective, he argued, you can interpret it any way you want. It can be actually used as evidence of the Confucianization of peasant culture, depending on how you want to label it. It depends on perspectives.

From an outsider's perspective, it can mean different things. The point he is trying to make about Chinese society is that everyone agrees that ancestor worship is an important feature of being Chinese. But what they believe about it is very different in different regions and different historical periods. It is *doing* it that is most critical, not necessarily carrying a set of ideas that everyone agrees upon.

Bol responded to this by saying that intellectual historians would be much more comfortable hearing Watson say this if he would bring in the various intellectual figures who offered intellectual justifications for orthopraxy, that is, the ideological justifications.

Joanna Handlin Smith questioned Tu as to whether Confucian self-identification in the twentieth century really was unprecedented. How would he, she asked, account for the swings from an easy tolerance of *sanjiao heyi (kuei-i)* "three teachings from one source" to periods of cleansing, such as represented by Zhang Lixiang (Chang Li-hsiang) or the Song neo-Confucians, who identified themselves as *ru*, distinct from Buddhists and Taoists. Is that not self-identification?

Tu responded by saying that if that was the impression that he had given, then he stands corrected.

Comparative Perspectives

TU WEIMING OFFERED a general summary, from a personal point of view, of some of the major issues raised during the workshop. This is not a summary of the discussions. Quite a number of points were made, not only from different specific regions but also from different levels of analysis from high culture to popular traditions. Rather, it is one person's observations of the kind of issues involved. The overall concern is really the story about the Confucian tradition and its modern transformation. The focus is not necessarily to develop an explanatory model of why industrial East Asia is so dynamic. Rather it is to have some sense of how this tradition we call the "Confucian tradition" developed in China, Korea, and Japan; how, as a response to the impact of the West, it underwent a major transformation (some people would even characterize it as disintegration); and how the Confucian motifs have reemerged in industrial East Asian societies. It is looming large in our minds. What is this animal in terms of its new representations of civilization?

Tu said that he looks at the Confucian tradition as a stream: it is dynamic and flows, with all kinds of different currents. One distinctive feature is its ability to interact with other traditions. Accordingly, we look at this story of Confucianism in a pluralistic context. It is very different from the story of Christianity, Islam, or Buddhism. Part of the reason is the Confucian *problematique*. It is the conception that the living, concrete human being is embedded in this world here and now and really will have to mobilize resources for self-understanding, for understanding of the world, for transforming the world, from within. Many major traditions in human history, what Karl Jaspers called the Axial Age, began with a transcendent vision of a world outside, of a spiritual sanctuary. One fascinating thing for Tu is that there is no counterpart of a Christian church, of a Buddhist temple, of a Taoist shrine, or a Judaic synagogue in a Confucian context. Therefore it is secular in a sense; it is embedded in the world here and now. And that embeddedness often gives us the impression, and this features very prominently in the Weberian interpretation, of adjustment to the world. The central *problematique* is "in the world, but not of the world." How will you be able to transform the world from within? What kind of symbolic and spiritual resources will you be able to tap in order to transform the world from within? Very early on, the central *problematique* for someone like Confucius was to accept the world order as still retrievable, as redeemable, and therefore meaningful, in a very basic sense, but yet, without being totally identified with power and relationships of the status quo. The project, then, is to moralize politics, to transform society through self-cultivation, through the development of a fellowship of Confucians, and accepting the power relationships as possible resources for transformation. Therefore, the symbolic resources, or the conceptual apparatuses that the Confucians used early on in trying to understand themselves, their relationship to the world, and ultimate concerns were very, very different. Not the contrast between the secular and the sacred, the profane and the sacred, the world here and the world beyond, but rather, inner and outer, the root and branch, self-cultivation and political order. This superficially optimistic view of the world is really predicated on a tragic sense that no matter how hard you try, the world can never be fully transformed. So very early on, in the Confucian paradox, every human being is perfectible (not just educable) through self-effort, so inherent in every human being is the possibility of self-transformation. But existentially, no human being, no matter how perfected, could afford not to continue to transform and develop himself or herself. And so we have this notion, on the one hand, that self-cultivation necessarily leads to social and political efficaciousness. At the same time, existentially, no matter how hard one tried, one would still have to continue to attempt to perfect oneself. This paradox was raised in the seventeenth century with the question whether Confucius, if he had lived a bit longer than seventy-two or seventy-three, would have tried harder, or whether he had reached the highest level of human perfection when he died. The consensus was that, of course, he had to try harder; he had to transform himself further. This gives us a very interesting problem. On the one hand, it is difficult to imagine anyone who is more Christian than Jesus or more Buddhist than the historical Sakyamuni. But it is quite conceivable that someone could be more Confucian than Confucius, more sagely than Confucius. Within the Confucian symbolism or tradition, Confucius himself was not considered as the highest level of perfection. The sage kings Yao and Shun and the Duke of Zhou were considered more perfect, more efficacious, more influential than Confucius. By Confucian standards, Confucius failed in a very fundamental way. Therefore, Tu does not think it totally ridiculous to say that Confucius was not the founder of the Confucian tradition, nor was he the highest manifestation of it. This provided a great deal of flexibility for further development, but created many problems for Confucians. One of these was that Confucians never developed an organized religion. Accordingly, membership within the Confucian community itself is always problematic. The assumption for the Confucian that every human being is in the process of learning how to be human has somehow been formed by the Confucian *problematique*. There is no membership for someone to become a member of in the Christian sense. So if we use Karl Rahner's category, everybody is an anonymous Confucian—everybody is a potential Confucian (Rahner maintained that there were quite a number of anonymous Christians). Of course, as Bol pointed out, if you look at the actual situation in China, the Confucians were those who in fact were members of the cultural elite, suggesting a notion of attainment, of achievement.

Now, if we look at the Confucian tradition as a stream, flowing through the Chinese historical landscape, a restless landscape, it started in the Shandong peninsula and gradually moved to the Central Plain and beyond. Recently a scholar in cultural geography in Fudan University has documented quite carefully, according to his own categories, how this tradition expanded geographically, moving beyond the Shandong peninsula to the Central Plain and on to other parts of China. It is a very interesting—and controversial—story. Now, Shimada Kenji, on his trip to China toward the end of the Cultural Revolution, argued that the Confucian tradition is not necessarily Chinese, because it is a manifestation of East Asian spirituality.

The second part of the story of Confucianism is that it emerged not just as one of the major intellectual traditions in China, but gradually entered three very important cultural areas, very distinct in cultural form from the central part of China: Korea, Vietnam, and Japan. One part of the story that has only recently begun to be fully explored—it is a complicated one—is the Mongolian, the Jurchen, and later the Manchu manifestations of the Confucian culture.

When we speak of the Confucian tradition as a common heritage in East Asia, one of the most fascinating stories is the emergence of Korea as the most thoroughly Confucianized state, from the fourteenth century to the early part of the twentieth century (the Choson dynasty, which was the longest in East Asian history, 1392–1910). There was a conscious attempt on the part of the political elite to Confucianize the society. The *yangban*, in fact, became much more powerful than the ruling minority, than the Korean king. The situation in Japan was much more complicated. Whether we can really speak of the Confucianization of the samurai class is debatable. Watanabe Hiroshi said that it is not possible for the samurai class, based as it is on the military spirit, to be thoroughly Confucianized. So, the argument runs, Japan can never be considered a Confucian society. But as Yamashita pointed out here, and also Tetsuo Najita at the University of Chicago, it is still possible to speak of the Confucian tradition as a common discourse about not just human relationships or socio-political organizations, but also understanding the world beyond. Emerging in this story, then, may be the minimum requirement of understanding the Confucian tradition: as a language of the moral order, of the moral community, as a common discourse. And you can use that language and identify yourself as a part of the universe or the linguistic world. Or you can use that language basically as a language of power. Tu believes that the language of power may be even more pervasive than the language of ethics and of self-understanding. In other words, it is possible to look at the Confucian tradition as a particular way in which a group of people that mobilized power through these kinds of symbolic resources developed a particular social structure, of which they were the beneficiaries. Confucianism as a language of power, as well as a language of ethics, that dominated the East Asian scene is one of the fascinating things about the emergence of Confucianism as a political ideology.

We are fascinated by the question of the primacy of the political order: the importance of the central government as the locus of power. Many people even believe that what Confucius really wanted to do was to become an official so that he could have enough power to transform society. Without being an official in the central government, he was unable to achieve this. Many people even believe that Confucius failed, not because such failure is embedded in the spiritual orientation, but instead because the time betrayed him. He was not able to become a powerful political leader.

Closely related to this is the notion that even the concept of being Chinese is not at all unconnected with the whole development of Confucian culture. Fung Youlan recently asked whether it was possible for us to understand the question of being Chinese without getting into the whole issue of the development of the Confucian tradition. From his point of view, the Confucian tradition, in fact, helped the Chinese to acquire a certain kind of cultural identity. The notion is that being Chinese is not just ethnically or regionally defined but is also culturally defined, and this partly stems from the Confucian tradition. This is a highly controversial topic.

There is no question about the primacy of the political order and the importance of the central government as the locus of power. We in East Asia as a whole, and in China in particular, conceive of the state not simply as a mechanism of control, but also as a form of moral order that can be coercive, sometimes even very coercive. In other words, the state, which in its emergence was totally independent of the Confucian tradition, became ritualized in such a way that it is understood not simply in the post-Machiavellian sense as a way of arranging power relationships, but also as an ethico-religious entity. The state is involved not only in developing economics and providing political order and social stability, but is also responsible for education. And in fact, the state became all-pervasive, if not omnipotent. The state felt that it had the right to interfere in many areas and provide leadership in many ways. The state often is perceived as the center of power. That is the expectation of the people, under the influence of Confucian culture, who wanted the state to perform a very important role. Ideally the leadership in the state is an exemplary leadership. But often, even though the state itself is staffed by people who are not particularly interested in Confucian rhetoric or self-cultivation, they feel both the obligation and right to provide themselves as exemplary leaders. This hubris of the state is very much informed by the pervasive Confucian legacy.

Tu singled out a particular area for focused investigation: the power of education, very much under the design of the state, to shape certain kinds of patterns of social interaction, or even recruitment. Of course, the examination system is an obvious example. The state is able to develop some kind of mechanism that gives it increasing power vis-à-vis the society at large. The center becomes so magnetic and powerful that all other forces in society, including commercial developments, will have to be somehow coordinated by the power of the state, through the recruitment of elite, based on the comprehensive vision of the state.

One curious thing in China, and applicable to Choson-dynasty Korea, was the inability of other social groups in society to develop an independent consciousness, that is, independent group solidarity based on a radically different intelligence, merchant consciousness, for example, or the consciousness of the workers or the peasants, independent of the power of the state. In China it is very difficult to find popular religious traditions or ideas that were totally independent. The rhetoric of peasant rebellions throughout Chinese history was informed by Confucian language. And and even Taoist and Buddhist leaders, in a way, used the same kind of language. Whether this is an indication of the Confucianization of Chinese society, or whether because the language is so flexible and so devoid of any detailed content it could be widely used, is a highly controversial issue. Not only is there no separation of the church and the state, therefore no spiritual sanctuary totally outside the world here and now, but also the whole state itself has assumed a very profound ethico-religious significance. And the society at large is suffused with these sorts of values that are widely used, even in the morality books.

It is fascinating to realize that lurking behind the scenes as background when the workshop began, but not fully articulated or developed, is that the

Confucian world in fact totally collapsed in the last one hundred fifty years. That background, Tu feels, informs continuously our uneasiness with these kinds of categories and ideas. So an important part of the story since the mid-nineteenth century is that a highly integrated universe based upon this Confucian symbolism that had lasted for a very long time suddenly collapsed because of the impact of the West. The notion of the rhetoric of wealth and power, as opposed to the rhetoric of moral order, was such that, for a while, some of the most brilliant minds in China believed that the fate of the Confucian tradition was sealed. This is still very much a controversial issue.

It is of very broad significance how a tradition that historically played such a major role in shaping the Chinese worldview could be abandoned by some of the most brilliant minds in China. Some believe, of course, that this is due to the impact of the West. In terms of the Chinese experience, it is almost as if the introduction of Buddhism and the Mongol invasions were compressed into one generation. This period, when China was reduced from the Middle Kingdom to "sickman of East Asia" in one generation, was the same period in which the United States emerged as a major international power. Also, we see very different reactions within East Asia to this impact. We are, Tu believes, still very much a part of this period, up to this date. Many scholars in the 1960s felt that with the impact of the West, all of East Asia would enter into a new era, that the age of Confucianism was gone forever, and that there is no need for us to understand the tradition in order to appreciate the dynamics of the modern transformation. But, part of the exercise here is to raise some questions about that perception: the sharp distinction between modernity, on the one hand, and traditional ideas on the other. So, the modern transformation of Confucian humanism, even though it may be of very limited intellectual consequence now, raises very interesting questions about the traditional motifs that have been explored in this workshop as ways of complexity of modern East Asia. Because of the collapse of the Confucian order, the coherence that many of the Confucian scholars observed as a historical phenomenon turned out to be problematic. There is no possibility of any reintegration of the Confucian world order: we have moved into a pluralistic society. From a pluralistic point of view, we learn that the kind of historical analysis that many had taken for granted turned out to be problematic as well. In other words, the exposure to complexity of the modern world forced us to reexamine the record of the Confucian tradition. At the same time, many of those involved in a study of the modern transformation now feel that they really need to explore the various kinds of categories within the Confucian tradition to understand the complexity of modern society, especially as manifested in East Asia.

So what we have, then, is the Confucian tradition and its modern transformation as one of the many possible stories about East Asia. It would also be possible, for example, to do this from a Buddhist or Taoist point of view. One of the most challenging things for Tu, he notes, is the argument that this story is not significant historically: that it is a social or a political construction. It is a rhetoric that was used to formulate various kinds of explanatory models, but it is not a reflection of actual social and political changes in terms of the historical moment. What the story is about is more like a modern, romantic reconstruction of a world that never existed. He will explore this challenge further. The Confucian story, the Confucian tradition needs to be deconstructed; we need to look at different kinds of social groups, political structures in order to understand what it is. This is a task not just for social scientists, but also for intellectual historians and scholars in many other fields.

All this is one extreme. The other extreme has resurfaced in China. That is, without being able to continue the Confucian rhetoric, with all its manifestations, the meaning of being Chinese is so fundamentally challenged that there is no way for the Chinese to connect themselves up with the traditional concept of being Chinese. In other words, there is a fundamental disintegration of the Chinese identity itself.

These two extremes present equal challenges to us, if we are interested in the Confucian tradition and its modern transformation. Quite a number of people may find that this not interesting enough or may find that the kind of explanatory power we can derive from this exploration may be insufficient to understand the dynamics of East Asia. His own view is that it is relevant and that the more he explores the topic, the more relevant it is. This is, though, he admits, only one person's view.

Stephen Graubard began by reminding the participants where they had stood on the evening they began the workshop. He had been, he remembered, very partial to Peter Berger's question to Ezra Vogel, "What *is* the *problematique?*" And it emerged from the discussion that the *problematique* was really taking up the Weber thesis—we all know the importance of Protestantism, of Calvinism really, in the development of capitalism—and asking whether these very successful East Asian societies are dominated by a Confucian ethic in some way so that the Confucian ethic has had that same kind of role. And several of us, including Graubard himself, he confessed, had no doubt that such an exercise would be an interesting one. Knowing something of the literature not only that Max Weber originated, but also the vast literature that grew out of that thesis, one had the feeling that it is a perfectly legitimate question that should, could, and might be asked, but he was less than overwhelmed by its possible uses.

What he heard Tu speaking of this morning was a much more interesting issue, one that reminded him of Shimuel Eisenstadt, who made a major contribution in the 1970s. He arrived at a moment when much of American social science was dominated by the idea of modernization. And the theme essentially was that there was a role that a society would have to adopt in order to become modern. The heretical question that he asked (and pointed fingers) really was the question that Tu is asking, in effect: In all of this modernization, in all of this looking simply at GNP, are we forgetting that two societies that may theoretically have the same GNP may have achieved that product by very different devices and remain fundamentally different? He put it very succinctly in an issue of *Daedalus* that Graubard still thinks is one of the most interesting ones we have, and one not irrelevant to what has been discussed here. In the winter 1973 issue, his article is entitled "Post-traditional Societies." What he asked was a simple question. The initial assumptions made in the early studies of modernization fail to explain the great variability of contemporary societies in their attempts to modernize themselves. Modernizing might have become a universal ambition, but it was being done in various ways with some reference to what these societies had been before. What he seems to have been really saying is that American social science had dwelled too much on the economic and too little on the intellectual and the social. He was interested in the transformations in Buddhism, in Islam, in Christianity itself, and in those things that could not be called religions at all. And how had they contributed to the modernity that these societies now expressed? It seemed to Graubard that this is what Tu is doing, but in a very different way. What Tu seems to be really talking about is that in the late nineteenth and early twentieth centuries there was the assumption, to use the Walter Bagehot phrase, that the "cake of custom" could be broken and that it could be replaced by something different that would eventually have a certain uniformity throughout the world. Now, rich countries are common in the world; what is interesting is what distinguishes some of these successes, and if one speaks of this, what does one have to speak of in terms of tradition and in terms of a thing called the state? What are the ideas, however attenuated, that existed in Confucianism and that somehow or other have survived and continue to inform what has happened? Tu seems to be saying, let us study Confucianism several hundred years ago, then reeling under the impact of the West, then let us study it as it emerges. This is a quite different approach, but the trajectory described is similar to that found within Islam: the encounter, the assumption that it was being superseded, and then the response. So what Tu seems to be saying is, let's not take a Western idea (not to maintain that Tu is arguing against a Weberian form of analysis) but look at the tradition over time. Such an approach, Graubard feels, has enormous importance for vast areas of the world other than East Asia.

Tu responded that during the period of the May Fourth Movement (this is the seventieth anniversary) some of the most brilliant intellectuals in China believed, as had Fukuzawa Yukichi before them in Japan, that the only process of modernization was the Anglo-American model. The Chinese made iconoclastic attacks on the tradition, including a total Latinization of Chinese. At present there is in Beijing another wave of wholesale Westernization. They are careful that this project of modernization will have to be debated and argued in Chinese; outsiders are not allowed into the picture. There is a fascination with nationalism and the modern transformation. Tu notes that he is reminded of the fact that in the 1960s, when theories of modernization, especially the structural-functional point of view, loomed very large in graduate studies in social science, the primordial ties considered absolutely essential for understanding tradition were to be relegated to the background. These include language, ethnicity, gender, land, and religion. Now in the late 1980s what we see is language featuring most prominently in the Third World, in England, France, Canada; ethnicity has been important since the 1970s; gender is now very important; the question of land and religion also. If we can look at the Confucian tradition from the perspective of the 1980s what is interesting is not simply its contribution to the economic dynamics of East Asia, but also how it is going to survive the democratization movement, how some of the directions that it originally took failed and now have become significant again, and things of that nature. In other words, the problem of transformation of tradition in modernity.

George De Vos said that he was a "left-over Durkheimian." One of its features was the nature of the sacred in society. Weber approached this from a very different angle than did Durkheim. In discussions of modernity, one of the main features is supposedly that the sacred turns toward the secular, there is a secularization of society that is a chief feature of modernity. Going back and making the case for Confucianism as a religion, De Vos explored what is sacred in Confucianism. Malinowski wrote a book called *Magic, Science, and Religion.* This work intrigues De Vos. In the transformation of magic into science, the concepts of mechanical causality feature prominently, and the quest for objectivity compels us to move beyond magical causality in an instrumental sequence, leading into scientific examination of mechanical causality. But then the term *religion* is left flapping by itself. What is the transformation within religion? Where do you go, from what to what, in a religious sequence? De Vos argued that religion has to do with intentional causality rather than mechanical causality. One of the features of Confucian thought was the moral universe. What is meant by a "moral universe"? In

Tokugawa Japan there was an attempt to reconcile what was seen as Western science, which was a mechanical form of causality, with the overarching concepts of a moral universe. What is sacred as a basis for considering Confucianism a religion? Now, obviously, in Confucianism very little attention is paid to forms of intentional causality that personify the supernatural. That is, one does not pay attention to the fact that there is an interference by some intentional being or beings in how things operate in the universe. The Confucian concern, nevertheless, is with intentionality, but intentionality is observed on the human plane. De Vos said that perhaps the transcendence that he would see if one goes from magic to science, if one wants to say that there is some sequential development in thought about spirituality, is the giving up of the supernatural and a concentration on the moral and the ethical as the remaining sacred in what is being looked at developmentally. He noted that he was working from a psychological developmental scheme with Piaget lurking in the background. In his concept of moral development, he goes from heteronomy to autonomy as human experience. Who said what is moral and where does it come from? Is it an absolute system or is it a legislative system? Does one get to legislative morality somewhere as a human form of morality? What is sacred in the United States? What is sacred in various states? De Vos's definition of the sacred is that it is what cannot be examined or taken apart. It is, in other words, what is a given that organizes and is a system of belonging that cannot be taken apart. If you do, then you get into nausea, Sartre's definition of meaninglessness, and so on. When you take apart the primary meaning and you lose it, then you lose your bearings and develop what Durkheim called anomie, that is, a lack of regulation, a lack of whatever is seen as harmony.

So, in the United States, the constitution is our sacred document and it is our legislative morality. In other words, if you look at the concept of the state through time, for example, at Shakespeare, he believed in a form of the state that was built around the concept of the divine right of kings. In other words, kingly succession was sacred, and the sense of moral order depended on a continuity of kingship. In a Chinese concept, the mandate of heaven *(tian-ming)*, there could be the necessity to examine dynastic succession in terms of whether the sacred was still embodied in the person exercising power. And if the sacred was not embodied in this person and he had lost it, then dynastic change was needed to reestablish the system and give a sense of the sacred in the power structure of the society. So the legitimacy, or concept of legitimacy, has to do with the fact that the sacred is embodied somewhere in the system, whether it is in a legal document or in a person. This cannot be questioned, cannot be taken apart, cannot be argued with, and is the source of belonging for those who constitute the society. This goes with ethnicity—which De Vos thinks of as a form of religion, if examined carefully. What is the ultimate belonging, ultimate sense of purpose? If a person is ethnic, then some of these definitions are to be found in the concept of what makes the person ethnic. The sense of power in this system is an intentional system. That is, power is intentional; it has to be exercised in terms of some kind of moral overarching system.

This brings up to De Vos the dilemma of Confucianism: where was it exercised? It had no church, De Vos argues, because the basis of Confucianism was the family. It was exercised in the meaning of the family and in the concept of family continuity. Robert Lifton has written a book on survivals, where he asks what ultimate religion is, and he comes to conclusions about some sense of continuity. Now the sense of continuity in the Christian trajectory is into eternity, and one's tight little ego goes on. In Buddhism, the ego disappears; there is continuity in the cosmos, but not on the basis of individual ego. In the Confucian system, the ego disappears into being part of a family. And it is the family continuity that was the essence of much Confucian thought: the being and the ultimate unquestioned, the sacred, was in family continuity, and the ancestral cult, in a sense, was the cult of continuity, into time and through time, and one's concept of the sacred and the unquestioned, and, in a sense, social purpose, or individual purpose, or purpose of self, was located within this trajectory through time, through the family as it was constituted. So the family shrine, whether in the house, or whether in Japan under Buddhist auspices, was still the concept of family continuity. Thus, De Vos argues, the religious sense in Confucianism has been located in the family continuity and could be transferred by overseas Chinese, because this continuity was kept. In Taiwan the question was, how can we reestablish ancestral places of being? Do we have to go back to China? Or can we relocate the family?

Confucianism, then, has been religion, argues De Vos, insofar as it has a concept of the sacred, there is an intentional causality lurking somewhere, rather than a mechanical causality. Now comes the dilemma. Confucianism seems to be losing out in China, De Vos feels. Students have become anomic and are looking for the sacred. They have taken on the concept of legislative morality as what they want to be the sacred, and they are giving up the concept of the family and its continuity. Therefore, De Vos is, ultimately, pessimistic about the continuity of Confucianism unless the family is maintained as part of the sacred.

Gilbert Rozman noted that the title of the session was "Comparative Perspectives" but that the group needed to move more quickly towards comparisons. What comparisons? How do we go about comparisons? The criticism of modernization theory, he would suggest, was a criticism of the Stalinist approach to Marxism rather than an analysis of what might be gained from a Gorbachev approach to Marxism, taking the most extreme forms. Also it is typical of a criticism of a comparative approach that emphasizes the patterns of modern development and how that affects different characteristics of society. Rozman argued that this kind of approach needs to be involved, whether it is modernization theory or not. We need to try to find some way of understanding whether, for example, Chinese patterns are compatible with changes in a modern society. De Vos came up with an answer, that he thought they might not be. That is the sort of question we must come back to, and in a historical perspective. What were the changes in Chinese, Japanese, and Korean societies? Rozman said that he would like a return to the sorts of themes that had come up the previous day when Vogel spoke of social mobility in education and MacFarquhar talked about moral education, and a series of themes like these as a basis for comparison. Tu also had introduced in this session some themes that should be developed in just this way, for example, when he had been speaking of the *yangban* versus the samurai versus the Chinese rulership. Rozman was struck by how what was hereditary in each society differed. In Japan it was the hereditary bureaucracy, essentially; while in Korea it was a hereditary social class; while in China it was a hereditary ruler in the imperial house. What are the implications of this?

Benjamin Schwartz spoke on the issue of religion and Confucianism. He said that he thinks that the traditional state in China had its very churchly aspect and mentioned a long treatise in the *Wenxian tongkao* on what the basic duties of the emperor were. If he really did it all, he would be spending most of his time offering sacrifices to the spirit of the mountain, to *tian*, and so on. So the state was secular in that it dealt with the kinds of secular issues that all states must deal with. But it was also religious even in a strong sense. The sacred can be found in the modern world, but it is essentially secular. The figure that looms large here is Descartes—not the man himself, but what became of him later. It is not just that it is a dualism, but that it is a strange kind of dualism: almost like two mutually exclusive monisms. There is the material world out there and there is the human subject here. So that everything that is not in the material world out there is projected back into the human subject. In Chinese, even in most of Confucian thought (Schwartz used to think Xun Zi was an exception, but a careful reading revealed otherwise), there is a deep faith—maybe it is unscientific—that the nonhuman universe is the source of all values, aesthetic, moral, and so forth. It is not a case of retrojecting, either into the human subject or some anthropocentric entity, like society. It seems to Schwartz that Durkheim's conception of the sacred is almost a religion of nationalism. The question of intentionality is also problematic. Schwartz would argue that there are some modes of religious thought in China that precisely do not emphasize intentionality. To this extent, on a superficial level they seem to resemble much of modern scientific philosophy of naturalistic thought. Take the *Yijing (I-ching)*. Human intentionality is almost regarded as a snake in the Garden of Eden. The universe worked beautifully; it was not meaningless. On the contrary, the fact that it was so routinized was the sign of its sacredness: the *wuwei* aspect of the universe. Maybe this is not, Schwartz argued, theistic, but it is profoundly religious. Religion to his mind is not just intentional theism. (But all this isn't really what I wanted to talk about!)

The word *modern* keeps coming up again and again. Evidently we do have to confront the question of what is at the heart of "modernism." Schwartz said that he had a bleak view of modernization theory himself, but still the unprecedented technico-economic development is one aspect of what happened in the West between the seventeenth and nineteenth centuries that has most impressed all the non-Western cultures. The notion that mankind had the capacity, which he had not realized, to do all these things, to increase wealth and power exponentially, was very striking. So one cannot get away from that aspect of modernization. But that notion that a state needs more wealth and power has become, with some exceptions, universalized. There are other things, though, of the modern West in the vaguer area of thought, since modernization is thought to involve modes of thought. Thus, the Cartesian split just mentioned is very important as a shared view. But not all of modern thought is necessarily coterminous with technico-economic development. What do we do with the Rousseauist element in modern Western thought, for example? It very much stressed socio-ethical values such as liberty, equality, democracy. There are, course, a great many unresolved contradictions between them, but these also made a considerable impression in the non-Western world. And many post-Enlightenment categories, whether we like it or not, have become part of the vocabulary of the intelligentsia in all the non-Western world. One thing, Schwartz noted, has always puzzled him about the concept of modernity: Is it a kind of "plateau concept"? That is, has mankind been struggling up a mesa only to reach a plateau and that's the end of it? Is modernity some unchanging thing? We are these days fumbling around with terms such as "postmodernity," a very feeble term. At least this indicates that in the modern world things have not stopped, that there are all kinds of changes. And the process goes on. Technico-economic changes began in the West, but there are things in other cultures that may be even more favorable than Western culture to further development.

Another thing that has happened is that (and this seems paradoxical) technico-economic development has forced us to face each other. We, sitting in America, have suddenly to think about what Iranian Shia teaching is. Alan Bloom made the point that one of the things that has happened is the inevitable confrontation with other cultures. To Schwartz's mind, this is a great opportunity. First of all, we now know that modernization in the narrow sense may very well be adaptable to non-Western cultures. We have neglected India in this workshop, but it is interesting that India has been much more sinuous than China in being able to take on certain devices of political democracy, pluralism. People said that India would fall apart, but it has not happened, at least yet! India may be sinuous toward the West in ways that China has not been. Meanwhile, we are getting into this "postmodern" world in which dialogues of cultures with their pasts and between each other is one of the great new, and exciting, opportunities, for it enlarges human experience. So unlike Alan Bloom, Schwartz finds it a welcome development.

Finally, concerning nationalism, Schwartz does not necessarily see it as a return to tradition. In some ways, it is a modern Western category. In this respect, the questions that Levenson raised seem quite relevant. Is it possible to have a fake traditionalism, in which the tradition of the past is praised only in order to draw nationalistic satisfaction?

Roderick MacFarquhar joked that while Tu Weiming has demonstrated repeatedly that as an individual he is quite humble, as a Chinese intellectual he displays all the characteristic arrogance of his class. MacFarquhar said that Tu views the collapse of the Confucian traditional order from the perspective of the elite. For Tu, the collapse of the Confucian state and world order seems to have caused great sensations of disequilibrium. The average Chinese peasant, though, has never concerned himself with the question of what it means to be Chinese.

Examining the family, one sees that what modern Confucians in East Asia have to worry about is not what it means to be Chinese or Japanese, but what it means to be an individual in a Confucian family. The average person worries about what it means to be an individual and in a Confucian family. While many in the West concern themselves with social order and stability, no political theorists spoke about the family as the basis for such order. Confucius and his followers got it right when they emphasized the role of the family as the root of stability.

Like Tu Weiming, the Chinese intellectuals have great problems with the May Fourth Movement because it is very difficult for them to reach back to the traditions that preceded the movement. What they must do, though, is examine the grass roots and construct the tradition from the bottom up, not from the top downward.

Peter Bol raised a set of issues that had been bothering him. Basically, it comes down to this: Under what circumstances should Confucianism be the focus for discussion of a group such as this? His questions have to do with issues of a comparative study of East Asia in the recent past. What comes out of this is that the PRC is the odd man out of Sinic civilization and is a great failure by many accounts. And Confucianism, in fact, would be part of the issue. If Confucianism is to be accounted as part of the reason for success in East Asia, then it must also be part of the problem. What Tu and MacFarquhar seem to be speaking of is a new elite redefinition of Confucianism as its value system. What is being proposed, in fact, is a radical redefinition of Confucianism. The two classical bases for Confucian values in the past were, Bol argued, their antiquity and the textual tradition. These are no longer part of the core curriculum, except for people like Tu Weiming, but not of Japanese and Chinese education. And second, ideas about heaven and earth *(tiandi)*. The notion of a rational, inherent, dynamic, organic order in the world. These are not incommensurate, but often they are in tension; this is frequently a traditional problem. Tu is not, Bol pointed out, holding up the authority of the sage kings and the sages as something you can believe in as primary meaning, sacred, authentic, and real. He is not holding up heaven and earth, the universe, as a source of values. Rather, we see an attempt to do precisely what MacFarquhar suggests, that is, to come up with a vision of Chinese society that will allow for a definition of a certain kind of ideology, of a certain set of values. It does not matter whether this is true to the Confucian tradition or not, because as long as modern intellectuals define it as the basis of their intellectual culture and their values, it will work. It is truly a modern transformation of the elite intellectual culture. In fact, we could throw Confucianism out the window and it would not matter. In fact, most Chinese intellectuals staying in the PRC would not accept the word *Confucianism* for it; they want to touch it, perhaps. But it seems to Bol that the conceptual problems involved in trying to derive a sense of what ought to be from what is are legion and manifest. One must be careful.

Ronald Dore made a plea not to have a discourse on discourse. When we speak of discourse, when talking even about tradition, we are conflating a large number of very different things: concepts, ways in which people divide up the physical and the moral world, principles, beliefs, cosmologies, and rituals. It is so much better to try to keep them separate. The sense in which one can talk of the samurai in the Tokugawa period as being Confucian was primarily in that when they faced moral dilemmas it was in terms of concepts derived clearly from Confucian discussions and in terms of principles of choice that they had explicitly been taught in the Four Books. Of these, the most important were almost entirely divorced from any sanctioning by the supernatural; it had become pretty completely a secular morality. These were most notably, Dore believes, the distinctions between public and private and the principle that where there is a clash, the principles of public morality should overcome those of private. It is often said that in Japan loyalty came before filial piety, whereas in China filial piety came first. Japan in the Tokugawa pretty well established the supremacy of the polity over the family. This is seen in the fact that in villages families did not defend delinquent members against the village community, come what may, that they were supposed to ostracize black sheep in order to maintain good standing in the village.

The impact of the West lay not only in bringing new ideas, but also in bringing new technology. The telegraph totally changed the relation between the provincial office and the central government. The *shidafu* sent out to the villages were no longer the same kind of creatures. They had to face the question of whether they should refer the problem to Beijing or not. The railway and the telegraph created the possibilities of social class movements and class consciousness. As Marx said in Europe, it was the railways that created classes, the fact that people in similar situations could move around, compare their lot, and create political parties. Together with the social invention of the strike, imported into China. That also changed the kinds of contingencies that the state had to deal with, which were simply not covered by the basic principles that had been at the center of ethical discussion. International trade gave an industrialist in Shanghai what the salt merchants never had, the choice of identifying himself with foreign interests as opposed to the interests of the state, as seeing himself as just one individual operating in the world market, as opposed to an individual who belonged to a particular polity.

Summary

TU WEIMING OPENED by making two short remarks. The first is that the distinction ought to be made between Confucian religiosity and the cult of Confucius. When he described the Confucian orientation as ethico-religious, without recognizing the spiritual sanctuary outside the world here and now, Tu referred to what he feels was a choice on the part of Confucius and Mencius not to develop a spiritual sanctuary as the justification for social transformation. This does not mean that Confucius or the Confucian tradition did not become deified. At one point in Chinese history, probably even as early as the Han, each of the counties was ordered to have a temple to Confucius, a *wenmiao*. The temple in Beijing has been rebuilt, by the way.

The other point that Tu wishes to clarify is that if we make a distinction between the cultural tradition of the modern East Asian intellectual and traditional culture, which Confucius is part of, it is important to point out that in the cultural heritage of the modern intellectual in East Asia, the modern West is an inalienable part and actually looms much larger than other traditional cultures, including Confucianism. For example, all the terms used in Chinese in trying to understand the world, all the technical terms, such as *zongjiao* "religion," *jingji* "economics," *zhengzhi* "politics," *shehui* "society," and so forth, all came from Japanese, and these terms in turn were translated by Japanese intellectuals in the late nineteenth and early twentieth centuries from Western terms. When at Peking University in 1985, Tu was explicit in telling his class that he was introducing a foreign cultural subject: Confucian philosophy. Tu recalled that he had gone on to inform the class that there are five great traditions that are particularly powerful in shaping the young minds in China. The first is the tradition of humiliation, ever since the mid-nineteenth century and the Opium War. The second tradition is the tradition of antitradition, of iconoclastic attacks on tradition. The third tradition is Marxism-Leninism. Next is the ten-year "rebellion is justified" tradition. The fifth is the tradition of reform of the last decade. All of these are intertwined. So the

Confucian tradition is a foreign culture, a distant echo in the minds of the people.

Chang Hao, picking up on Schwartz's comments in response to De Vos (who had to leave after the last session), said that we should be reminded again of the plea voiced earlier of the need to be aware of the complexities of the Confucian tradition with regard to the problem of sacredness, as well as to many other things. De Vos has emphasized the family as the sole locus of sacredness and a possible source of continuity. Now, Schwartz has pointed to the sacred nature of the political order, especially the cosmological king.

Chang suggests yet another source of sacredness in China: the individual, as a vehicle of the encompassing whole, of the *tian* and the *di*. This kind of image of individual as a source of sacredness had already emerged before Confucius. In the *Zuozhuan* there is a famous conversation quoted many times by many modern Chinese scholars, including Hu Shih and Ch'ien Mu, emphasizing the sacredness of the individual as a vehicle of the beyond. The context of the conversation is that an eminent figure in the late Zhou period asked another eminent figure about the nature of immortality. The answer given was that there were three forms. One is to have great achievement; the second is to develop your virtue; and the third form is to leave behind your work of literary merit *(ligong, lide, liyan)*. Even though you die, these things will go on. In this we find, Chang argues, a reference to individuals maintaining continuity, even when the physical self has passed away. This idea of the individual as the vehicle of the larger whole, and therefore becoming a source of sacredness, was further developed in the Confucian tradition, especially the neo-Confucian tradition. This is a central element in, for example, the *Daxue* and the *Zhongyong*. They emphasize that individuals, through moral cultivation, can also be the recipient of *tianming*. In sum, the Confucian tradition contains diversified sources of sacredness, indicating the complexity of the Confucian heritage. These forms can be used as sources of continuity and as symbolic resources for building up a new identity in the future.

Henry Rosovsky said that he felt that this morning's discussion was very difficult for an economist to follow. It seems that whenever Schwartz invokes the term "economics" and speaks of "technico-economics," a frown comes over his face as if he were drinking a spoonful of castor oil. (Not at all! Schwartz responded.) Mark Twain once asked if it is better to say nothing and to have people think you are a fool, or to open your mouth and prove it? Rosovsky wanted to make a plea not to abandon the Weberian question, and certainly not to deal with it as dismissively as Graubard did. He feels that the Weberian question remains fundamentally important, unanswered, and very significant as we contemplate one thrust of this whole project.

First of all, why some countries have grown more rapidly than others and why some have failed to develop is a question that has not been satisfactorily answered, neither by economists nor by other social scientists. Furthermore, it is generally believed that East Asia will be the most rapidly growing part of the world. This raises a very interesting question: What unites East Asia? What is the common denominator? It has been suggested that the only thing that unites East Asia is soy sauce and chopsticks. Perhaps one can also introduce a bit of Confucianism into this.

The other important question is related to this. That is, orthodox economic assumptions do not seem to produce the predicted results. It is well known now that the economies of the countries that we have discussed—especially Japan and the Gang of Four, excluding the PRC for the moment—are full of oligopolies, full of concentration, full of restrictions of various kinds. All of that should produce, in terms of received conventional economic wisdom, negative results when, in fact, they produce obviously positive results.

Rosovsky is not, he noted, very fond of much that Chalmers Johnson has to say about these things, but he must be given credit for the attack he has mounted on economists, which is in many ways well deserved. All of this could be put under the Weberian question, and it is hoped that it will not disappear as the analysis of these issues proceeds.

Stephen Graubard responded that he agreed with Rosovsky more than he realized. He said that he had not at all intended to dismiss the Weberian hypothesis, but had been trying to reflect the conversation of the first afternoon and evening. Second, if you do follow the Weberian model, you will very quickly have a literature rather like that which has followed Weber, in which there will be discussion of all the other places having rapid growth that are not, in fact, ultimately explicable by this alone. He would like to emphasize particularly that he worries when he reads things such as the recent MIT study on productivity in America. It argues as if the problem is that the Americans are not able to do any number of things that the Japanese do. What it does not argue sufficiently is that there is a vast other world doing many of these things, sometimes almost as rapidly. Little attention, for example, is paid to individual countries in Europe (as opposed to the EC as a whole), for example. He is trying to remind us that the present phenomenon of rapid growth in many parts of the world really ought to concern us, though we should pay particular attention to East Asia, because it is so totally unanticipated.

Rosovsky responded that, supposing there are different explanations for different parts of the world, getting it right of the billion-plus people residing in East Asia would not be a minor achievement.

Benjamin Schwartz responded that he had not intended to be condescending toward economics and said that he appreciated many of the benefits conferred by technico-economic growth. But, like so many human phenomena, it has its ambivalences. He does not feel that the evil consequences that have emerged are any less real than the good ones. And furthermore, what worries him in the long run is the idea of unlimited anything. There is also the notion that all other problems are just a spin-off. It worries him, for instance, to hear that what becomes of the family in the United States will depend totally on what line technico-economic growth takes. If the family is really good, then maybe we should shape the technico-economic growth to meet its needs. In other words, the notion that everything should be ancillary to technico-economic growth worries him. He still would maintain that he is not a Luddite!

Ronald Dore said that, in a way, the diffusion of modern industrialism is not problematic; it is to be expected. The form of the Weberian question that remains interesting to Dore is why it diffused so much more rapidly and efficiently in East Asia than in India or in Indonesia, say. Then, if one is doing comparative studies to answer this question, it is not the West and East Asia that one should compare, but instead East Asia and India or Indonesia.

Tu said he felt prompted to share a thought. For about ten years a group in Europe with Wolfgang Schluchter at the University of Heidelberg and Shimuel Eisenstadt involved as well, has tried to reopen the Weberian question. The term they use now is trying to "de-Parsonianize" Weber. So there are two Weber theses, both very interesting. One is the question of finding the functional equivalent of Protestantism. That question has a variety of conceptual difficulties. The other issue is to question the relationship between ethico-religious concerns, on the one hand, and economic performance, on the other. In other words, introducing the cultural factor as a way of understanding complex transformation. Peter Berger is very involved in this, to the extent that he formed an institute studying economic culture. The strategy used by some of these European scholars, including Schluchter (who is also close to Habermas) is to try to look at the Weberian question from the perspective of Karl Jaspers. They wish to examine how all these major civilizations, including Hinduism, Buddhism, Confucianism, and Islam, actually developed, not just spiritually, but socially, politically, and economically as well, and try to see whether Weber as a comparativist (rather than as a narrow-minded modernist) is relevant. It now seems that we see the possibility of more than one form of modernity, despite the fact that the modern Western form probably generated this whole process.

Lin Tongqi spoke on the possibility of the development of Confucianism in China. During the past six years, there had been a debate on this topic in China. The output of this has been more than one thousand articles. In general, in the field of Chinese philosophy there are three trends. One is the revival of the study of Confucianism. The second is the enormous influx of Western thought. The third is the decline and readjustment of Marxism. These three trends intertwine and make the situation fluid and difficult to analyze.

Lin noted that there had been many seminars on the upsurge of interest in Confucianism. There was a seminar where Cai Shangshi, a scholar known for his anti-Confucian positions, became very isolated. All the other participants criticized him. This illustrates the process of the reevaluation of Confucius in China, which began around 1980. This is not to say that outside such seminars a very powerful strain of antitraditionalism does not exist. Another point illustrating the trend is the establishment of the International Academy of Chinese Culture (Zhongguo Wenhua Shuyuan), set up under the sponsorship of Peking University in 1985. It was approved by authority as high as the secretariat of the Central Committee of the Chinese Communist Party. This academy sponsored four lectures. The first had an attendance of three hundred; the second, third, and fourth had thousands of scholars, students, and graduate students in attendance. This academy also provided a correspondent program that has managed at least twelve thousand students. Every province has a quota of at least five hundred students who can apply for admission. All this shows that in the past few years there has been enormous interest in Confucianism in China.

An interesting fact is that the older scholars who specialize in Confucianism tend to be anti-Confucian. For example, there is a very big project sponsored by the State Education Commission, led by two or three major scholars. Between them and their younger assistants there is a gap: the younger ones are much more positive about Confucianism. So there is a trend in China, just starting, developing on the intellectual scene, toward interest in Confucianism; it may not be the dominant trend, but rather one of many in the future.

There is a methodological problem that is very important currently. It involves the question of *neisheng* and *waiwang* ("inner sageliness" and "outer kingliness" as a defining characteristic). Can the inner and outer be separated? Which should enjoy priority? This whole issue is very important if one wants to discuss Confucianism with Chinese scholars.

Peter Bol asked Lin if he would want other people to call him a Confucian.

Lin responded that he would not and that very few Chinese would like to be called Confucian, although they share, even embrace some of the Confucian values. The term "Confucian" is not very viable in China, probably due to the May Fourth stigma.

Samuel Yamashita said that he found the language that was being used interesting. There had been the center and periphery, the high and low, the language of pluralism, the metaphor of the stream. He said that he would like to suggest another possible category: borderlands, or periphery. If it is the case that our interest is the success of the Four Dragons and Japan, then it might be interesting to consider the transformation of Confucianism in the borderlands as a specific kind of problem. It is in those places that the Confucian language is transformed in very interesting ways: appropriations, synthetic combinations, and so forth. Confucianism survives in those places sometimes in nontextual ways, in families, in values, in rituals. It might be interesting to look at those configurations in the borderlands in developing an explanation of their success.

Tu remarked that in 1919 the notion of the center radiating outward to the periphery was taken for granted. But for the last seventy years we have seen the periphery challenging the center, in many, many ways, in Canton, in the Pacific area, and the overseas Chinese communities throughout the world.

Thomas Gold returned to the Weber question. One thing he likes about Weber's approach is his refusal to discuss laws of social development and his emphasis on configurations. One way Gold has tried to approach this issue at hand is to try to deconstruct the different aspects of what we call Confucianism. One of the things Weber stressed was the carriers of different sorts of values and worldviews and his famous notion of how sometimes ideas play the role of switchman in history. But there are social forces that carry these ideas. When we look at *The Religion of China,* we tend to emphasize the discussion of the intellectual essence of Confucianism, but often forget the passage at the very end of the work where he points out that even though capitalism did not originate in China, given the proper circumstances it would catch on like wildfire. Gold takes this to mean that once these socio-structural obstacles are removed, then there is no problem at all with the development of capitalism. So Gold does not see the whole issue as a great mystery; he feels that the possibilities of East Asian capitalist growth are already explicit in Weber's work.

In the study of development there is, said Gold, a real impasse. In the period after World War II, there was an emphasis on studying the Third World, or underdeveloped areas, to try to analyze what their potential might be for development and how we could remove the obstacles to development so there could be a diffusion from the West, especially the United States. This was a Parsonization (and misreading on certain things) of Weber. In the 1960s and 1970s, when modernization did not occur, the emphasis in the field shifted to explanations of why these countries were failing. Now there is an attempt to explain why some have succeeded after all. One of the major splits in development theory is between those scholars who study East Asia and those who study Latin America. The former, by and large, maintain that the reason the East

Asian dragons and Japan have succeeded has something to do with culture, in addition to various other factors. Specialists on development in Latin America, on the other hand, still blame the failure of their region on imperialism and not culture. In the East Asian field there are two emphases: one on culture and the other on the state. Some people see East Asian development as becoming a new paradigm in the field, replacing modernization theory and dependency theory with a state theory, bringing the state back in. There is now a reaction against this as well, saying that you cannot just look at the state, but must also understand that development has something to do with the interrelationship between state and society. Society can be something of an autonomous actor, given certain exigencies. But how to understand society and the "black box" of culture? Latin American specialists just dismiss it as a "residual category." Hence, Gold feels that conferences of this sort can make a real contribution toward understanding culture as an ongoing, living, dynamic thing and apprehending how it relates to certain social factors.

Roderick MacFarquhar pointed out that even within the East Asian field there are those who do not wish to deal with culture.

Gold hastened to agree. He joked that in meetings the other participants often seem to be thinking, "Here he goes again."

Rosovsky noted that there was some very interesting work going on even among economists on this issue. Aoki at Stanford has done work on the "J firm" (in Japan) and brings in a number of cultural factors.

Tu mentioned the project at the East-West Center addressing this issue, with Robert Dernberger from the University of Michigan.

MacFarquhar said that what was happening in China during the democracy movement in Beijing was yet another example of the inability of the rigid, Confucian-type state structure to deal with the forces of society that it has itself unleashed in the modernization process. In China the central state command methods of Stalinism have been combined with a traditional Chinese state structure. When that state structure and its manipulators find they cannot do it and they start to unleash social forces, as Deng Xiaoping has done over the last ten years, they then find that the state structure is too rigid to cope with the forces they have unleashed. It is that clash that is currently being played out.

Bol confessed that as a historian who works in Tang and Song history, and intellectual history at that, he was not terribly moved by the question of modernization, although he recognizes its importance to a great many other scholars. An issue that runs through much of the proceedings is: Japan is so successful in competition, so why is not China as well? And what are the resources China can draw upon to become successful? Bol said that he hopes

conferences such as this can help answer a further question, which is, what are
the Chinese elites trying to do, apart from modernizing? Are they, in fact,
committed to making China a competitive state? Which groups are? Another
issue, brought up by Gold, is that of culture. It would be interesting to have
social scientists speak on what the modern Chinese conception of culture is.
Or more broadly, what are the categories they use for thinking about social
and economic life? How do they divide things up?

James Watson said that, on the question of economic development in
Chinese society, one of the things that had impressed him on his first visit to
the central and northern areas of China was the fact (widely known, but
difficult to comprehend without firsthand travel) that there are many Chinas.
The areas developing are primarily the Jiangnan and Pearl River delta region.
There are many, many parts of China that would in every respect fit the Latin
American model. We need to remember that it is not just Chinese culture that
we are describing, but instead, certain regional, dynamic subcultures.

Tu had some closing thoughts. First he addressed himself to Bol's challenging question concerning the redefinition of Confucian humanism as a reflection of the elite mentality in trying to redefine the socio-political order. The
question is whether the best way to get at the Confucian question is to take
the state as the locus of power. If the state is in the process of disintegration,
then the Confucian persuasive power wedded to a particular kind of ruling
elite will also be totally undermined. One result of this workshop has been to
highlight the need for a thorough examination of this issue. There is no
question that when Tu came to Harvard and studied under Fairbank and
others, he learned that you have to understand Confucianism if you want to
understand the modern transformation; Confucianism is a political ideology.
So there, in a number of volumes, a collective effort of leading scholars in North
America tried to address this issue: *The Confucian Persuasion, Confucianism in
Action, Confucian Personalities,* and *Chinese Culture and Institutions.* These
volumes were all very much focused on the Confucian tradition as a form of
political ideology. Starting in 1966 another series of conferences was organized,
basically under the leadership of de Bary and Wing-tsit Chan. The goal was to
speak of the neo-Confucian period, not necessarily in terms of political
ideology, but in terms of self-cultivation. These resulted in such works as *Self
and Society in the Ming, The Unfolding of Neo-Confucianism, Principle and
Practicality, The Rise of Neo-Confucianism in Korea,* and more recently, a series
of works on Confucian education. In addition, there is a project in which
Rozman is involved, along with Marius Jansen and others, trying to understand
modernization comparatively in China, Japan, and Korea, and the Confucian
issue understood in terms of modernization.

There are two very different approaches to Confucianism, but Tu believes that they come together in the end. These first is an attempt to look at the Confucian tradition in terms of the role of the state. The other is to look at Confucianism as an ideology of the cultural elite. Members of the cultural elite and the ruling minority are two overlapping categories, but they must be distinguished. There are those people who, in fact, were instrumental in developing the Confucian ideology as a mechanism of control. One of the most interesting examples of this was the rule of the Manchus. If one looks at the emperors of the Qing as opposed to those in the Ming or the Song, they really met the basic requirements of Confucian rulership. Kangxi, Yongzheng, and Qianlong were outstanding Confucian leaders. They were Confucian and very powerful; they undermined the power of the Han cultural elite to assert themselves as carriers of the Confucian message. It was during the Manchu state that the politicization of Confucian moral persuasion became complete, and that legacy continues. The self-image of the state to Deng Xiaoping and others is such that they really consider themselves to be in control, not only of the political arena, but also of the moral and the ideological arenas as well. Mao was really the combination of everything, all kinds of leadership: symbolic, moral, political, economic.

MacFarquhar interjected that he was also a rebel leader, unfortunately for China.

Tu continued, yes, also a rebel leader. Under this pervasive pattern, which is hierarchically structured, there is an inseparability of morality on the one hand and politics on the other.

However, Tu noted, this meeting had tended to suggest that there were other sides to the Confucian persuasion that need to be examined. There are internal conflicts and tensions. One, of course, is the family, located not in the political, but the social arena. That social arena of the family has a life of its own, its sense of power, its sense of sacredness. The image of the family is very pervasive in East Asia as a whole.

Schwartz interjected that he saw another image in the student hunger strikers in Tiananmen Square that was very Confucian. Showing deep sincerity about their issue and the force of their manifestation of *meite* ("lovely virtue") seems to echo Confucian tradition.

Tu continued that once one does not simply locate the Confucian tradition in the political arena, there is the family center, which is a social arena. But an issue that has emerged here is what our understanding of the cultural elite really is. What are the resources they tap in order to formulate their self-understanding? A historical note: when Mencius approached the political elite, he was arrogant. Sima Guang, already in the Song dynasty, could not really understand how he could have been so arrogant. Mencius felt that he represented a cultural tradition, independent of political power. Second, he felt that he represented the conscience of society, and therefore the populace as a whole, whereas he saw the leader of the state as basically representing something like a private interest of a small group. In addition, there was a transcendent referent; he felt that he was in keeping with the mandate of heaven. In other words, his strength as an engaged intellectual lay in the cultural tradition, the populist basis of social conscience, and the transcendent referent. All these converged in terms of dignity of the person through self-cultivation. It was felt as something achieved, an attainment, not something born with. The current student demonstrations are interesting. There is a very long history in China of student demonstrations, from the Han dynasty against corrupt officials, again in the Ming. They had the power of virtue, moral power. The current student movement represents the conscience of the society as a whole, as against the state, which is seen as having its own narrow private interests at heart. The term *Zhongguohun* is used as well and has transcendent referent. The *tianming* issue is quite clear. They are telling the leadership that it has lost the mandate, not because it does not have real power, but because the structure itself is totally illegitimate, because the leaders had failed to become accountable. These kinds of themes and ideas are still vibrating powerfully.

Glossary

"Analects" (Lun Yü)	論語
Bo Yang	柏楊
"Bunge Shunju" (Japanese magazine)	文藝春秋
Cai Shangsi (Ts'ai Shang-ssu)	蔡尚思
chaebol (K)	財閥
Chang Chun-mai (Zhang Junmai)	張君邁
Chang Hao (Zhang Hao)	張灝
Chang Lü-hsiang (Zhang Luxiang)	張履祥
Chen Xia	陳霞
Cheng Chung-ying (Cheng Zhongying)	成中英
chengren (ch'eng-jen)	成人
Ch'ien Mu (Qian Mu)	錢穆
Chiang Ching-guo (Jiang Jingguo)	蔣經國
chonin bunka (J)	市井文化
Chon Tu-hwan (K)	全斗煥
Dasai Shundai (J)	大宰春台
Daxue (Ta-hsüeh)	大學
dangxiao (tang-hsiao)	黨校
Deng Xiaoping	鄧小平
di	地
Donglin (Tung-lin)	東林
Fan Zhongyan (Fan Chung-yen)	范仲淹
Fang Tung-mei (Fong Dongmei)	方東美
Fang Keli	方克立

Note: All glossary entries are listed according to the alphabetic order of Hanyu pinyin, except proper names and names and terms in Japanese and Korean (identified by J and K following the word).

fengsheng yusheng dushusheng   風聲雨聲讀書聲　聲聲入耳
    shengsheng ruer
fukoku kyohei (J)   富國強兵
Fukuzawa Yukichi (J)   福澤諭吉
Feng Yulan (Feng Youlan)   馮友蘭
fuqiang (fu-ch'iang)   富強
guanxi   關係
Han Feizi (Han Fei-tzu)   韓非子
He Shang   河殤
Ho Lin (He Lin)   賀麟
Hsiung Shih-li (Xiong Shili)   熊十力
Hsü Fu-kuan (Xu Fuguan)   徐復觀
Hu Shi (Hu Shih)   胡適
"Huangming Jingshi Wenbian"   皇明經世文編
    (Huang-Ming ching-shih wen-pian)
hyanggyo (K)   鄉校
Ito Jinsai (J)   伊籐仁齋
jiashi guoshi tianxiashi shishi guanxin   家事國事天下事　事事關心
Jiangnan (Ch'iang-nan)   江南
jingji (ching-chi)   經濟
jingshi (ching-shih)   經世
jingshi jimin (ching-shih chi-min)   經世濟民
Kangxi (K'ang Hsi)   康熙
Kang Youwei (K'ang Yu-wei)   康有爲
kaozheng (k'ao-cheng)   考證
keju   科舉
Kiho   畿輔
Kim Song-il (K)   金成一
"Kojiki" (J)   古事記
kokugakusha (J)   國學者
Kuomintang (KMT, Guomindang)   國民黨
Lee Kwan Yew (Li Guangyao)   李光耀
Lee Teng-hui (Li Denghui)   李登輝
Li Ao   李敖
licai jiushi shengcai (li-tsai chiu-shi   理財就是生財
    sheng-tsai)
lide (li-te)   立德
ligong (li-kung)   立功
liyan (li-yen)   立言
Liang Shu-ming (Liang Shuming)   梁漱溟

Lin Tongqi	林同奇
Liu Shu-hsien (Liu Shuxian)	劉述先
Liu Yü-yun (Liu Yuyun)	劉毓雲
luan	亂
meide (mei-te)	美德
minzu (min-tzu)	民族
minzuhun	民族魂
Mou Tsung-san (Mou Zongsan)	牟宗三
neisheng	內聖
"Nihon Shoki" (J)	日本書紀
Nishi Yamane (J)	山根西
O Yo-mei (see Wang Yangming)	
Ogyu Sorai (J)	狄生徂徠
Pak Chung-hee (K)	朴正熙
Pang Pu	龐朴
peiyang (p'ei-yang)	培養
Qianlong (Ch'ien Lung)	乾隆
Qing (Ch'ing)	清
Ro Tae-woo (K)	盧泰愚
ru (ju)	儒
rujia (ju-chia)	儒家
sangang	三綱
"Sanguo Yani" (Sanguo yani)	三國演義
sanjiao heyi (san-chio ho-i)	三教合一
shanghui	商會
shangxia zhihfen (shang-hsia chih-fen)	上下之分
shehui	社會
shi (shih)	士
shidafu (shih-ta-fu)	士大夫
shuerbuzuo (shu-erh pu-tsuo)	述而不作
shushin (J)	修身
sike (ssu-k'e)	四科
Sima Guang (Ssu-ma Kuang)	司馬光
Sima Qian (Ssu-ma Ch'ien)	司馬遷
Song (Sung)	宋
Songgyun'gwan (K)	成鈞館
sowon (K)	書院
Sun Yat-sen (Sun Zhongsan)	孫逸仙 (孫中山)
Syngman Rhee (K)	李承晚
Taixue (T'ai-hsüeh)	太學

Tang (T'ang)	唐
T'ang Chün-i (Tang Junyi)	唐君毅
ti (t'i)	體
tian (t'ien)	天
Tiananmen (T'ien-an-men)	天安門
tiandao (t'ien-tao)	天道
tiandi (t'ien-ti)	天地
tianming (t'ien-ming)	天命
Tokugawa bakufu (J)	德川幕府
tokushitsu (J)	特質
Tosan	陶山
Tu Wei-ming (Du Weiming)	杜維明
waiwang	外王
Wang Anshi (Wang An-shih)	王安石
Wang Mang	王莽
Wang Yangming	王陽明
wenmiao	文廟
"Wenxian Tongkao" (Wen-hsien t'ung-k'ao)	文獻通考
Wu Han	吳晗
wuwei	無爲
xiao (hsiao)	孝
xinxue (hsin-hsüeh)	心學
Xuehaitang (Hsüeh-hai-t'ang)	學海堂
Xun Zi (Hsun Tzu)	荀子
Yamasaki Anzai (J)	山崎闇齋
Yan Fu (Yen Fu)	嚴復
"Yantielun" (Yen-tieh lun)	鹽鐵論
Yang Tsung Rong	楊聰榮
yangban (K)	兩班
Yang Tingyun (Yang Tingyun)	楊廷筠
"Yijing" (I-ching)	易經
Yi T'oegye (K)	李退溪
Yi Yulgok (or Yi I) (K)	李栗谷 (李珥)
Yongnam (K)	嶺南
Yongzheng (Yung Cheng)	雍正
Yu Kil-chun (K)	俞吉濬
Yulim (K)	儒林
Yü Ying-shih (Yu Yingshi)	余英時
zhengzhi (cheng-chih)	政治

zhishi fenzi (chih-shih fen-tzu)	知識分子
Zhongguohun	中國魂
Zhongguo Wenhua Shuyuan	中國文化書院
"Zhongyong" (Chung-yung)	中庸
Zhou (Chou)	周
Zhou Enlai (Chou Enlai)	周恩來
"Zhouli" (Chou-li)	周禮
Zhu Xi (Chu Hsi)	朱熹
Zhu Xiaokang	朱小康
Zhuang Zi (Chuang Tzu)	莊子
zongjiao	宗教
"Zuozhuan" (Tso-chuan)	左傳

Index

The East-West Center

The U.S. Congress established the East-West Center in 1960 to foster mutual understanding and cooperation among the governments and peoples of the Asia-Pacific region, including the United States. Principal funding for the Center comes from the U.S. government, with additional support provided by private agencies, individuals, and corporations and more than twenty Asian and Pacific governments.

The Center promotes responsible development, long-term stability, and human dignity for all people in the region and helps prepare the United States for constructive involvement in Asia and the Pacific.